Victoria Cann is Lecturer in Humanities at the University of East Anglia. Her research is concerned with the processes through which identity is reproduced, and feminist politics more broadly. She has published on the topic of gendered audiences, identity politics and the politics of representation. She teaches gender, media and cultural politics in the Interdisciplinary Institute for the Humanities at the University of East Anglia. She also undertakes a range of feminist engagement work in the community, such as her role with Day of the Girl, Norwich.

'Drawing on ambitious ethnographic research with over 100 British youth, Victoria Cann explores how taste articulation functions to regulate and reproduce gender norms within teenage culture in the UK. Through her astute analysis of gendered tastes from football to One Direction and gendered practices from "shunning" to "fangirling", Cann guides the reader through the halls of the contemporary high school, interrogating the relationship between gender, youth, and cultural tastes that play out there. Indeed, *Girls Like This, Boys Like That* reminds us that youth taste matters, and that we should be paying more attention.'

Jessalynn Keller, Assistant Professor Department of Communication, Media and Film University of Calgary, Canada

Library of Gender and Popular Culture

From *Mad Men* to gaming culture, performance art to steam-punk fashion, the presentation and representation of gender continues to saturate popular media. This new series seeks to explore the intersection of gender and popular culture, engaging with a variety of texts – drawn primarily from Art, Fashion, TV, Cinema, Cultural Studies and Media Studies – as a way of considering various models for understanding the complementary relationship between 'gender identities' and 'popular culture'. By considering race, ethnicity, class, and sexual identities across a range of cultural forms, each book in the series will adopt a critical stance towards issues surrounding the development of gender identities and popular and mass cultural 'products'.

For further information or enquiries, please contact the library series editors:

Claire Nally: claire.nally@northumbria.ac.uk
Angela Smith: angela.smith@sunderland.ac.uk

Advisory Board:

Dr Kate Ames, Central Queensland University, Australia

Prof Leslie Heywood, Binghampton University, USA

Dr Michael Higgins, Strathclyde University, UK

Prof Åsa Kroon, Örebro University, Sweden

Dr Niall Richardson, Sussex University, UK

Dr Jacki Willson, Central St Martins, University of Arts London, UK

**Library of Gender
& Popular Culture**

Published and forthcoming titles:

The Aesthetics of Camp: Post-Queer Gender and Popular Culture
By Anna Malinowska

Ageing Femininity on Screen: The Older Woman in Contemporary Cinema
By Niall Richardson

All-American TV Crime Drama: Feminism and Identity Politics in Law and Order: Special Victims Unit
By Sujata Moorti and Lisa Cuklanz

Bad Girls, Dirty Bodies: Sex, Performance and Safe Femininity
By Gemma Commane

Beyoncé: Celebrity Feminism in the Age of Social Media
By Kirsty Fairclough-Isaacs

Conflicting Masculinities: Men in Television Period Drama
By Katherine Byrne, Julie Anne Taddeo and James Leggott (Eds)

Fathers on Film: Paternity and Masculinity in 1990s Hollywood
By Katie Barnett

Film Bodies: Queer Feminist Encounters with Gender and Sexuality in Cinema
By Katharina Lindner

Gay Pornography: Representations of Sexuality and Masculinity
By John Mercer

Gender and Austerity in Popular Culture: Femininity, Masculinity and Recession in Film and Television
By Helen Davies and Claire O'Callaghan (Eds)

The Gendered Motorcycle: Representations in Society, Media and Popular Culture
By Esperanza Miyake

Gendering History on Screen: Women Filmmakers and Historical Films
By Julia Erhart

Girls Like This, Boys Like That: The Reproduction of Gender in Contemporary Youth Cultures
By Victoria Cann

The Gypsy Woman: Representations in Literature and Visual Culture
By Jodie Matthews

Love Wars: Television Romantic Comedy
By Mary Irwin

Masculinity in Contemporary Science Fiction Cinema: Cyborgs, Troopers and Other Men of the Future
By Marianne Kac-Vergne

Moving to the Mainstream: Women On and Off Screen in Television and Film
By Marianne Kac-Vergne and Julie Assouly (Eds)

Paradoxical Pleasures: Female Submission in Popular and Erotic Fiction
By Anna Watz

Positive Images: Gay Men and HIV/AIDS in the Culture of 'Post-Crisis'
By Dion Kagan

Queer Horror Film and Television: Sexuality and Masculinity at the Margins
By Darren Elliott-Smith

Queer Sexualities in Early Film: Cinema and Male-Male Intimacy
By Shane Brown

Steampunk: Gender and the Neo-Victorian
By Claire Nally

Television Comedy and Femininity: Queering Gender
By Rosie White

Television, Technology and Gender: New Platforms and New Audiences
By Sarah Arnold

Tweenhood: Femininity and Celebrity in Tween Popular Culture
By Melanie Kennedy

Women Who Kill: Gender and Sexuality in Post-Feminist Film and Television
By David Roche and Cristelle Maury (Eds)

Wonder Woman: Feminism, Culture and the Body
By Joan Ormrod

Young Women in Contemporary Cinema: Gender and Post-feminism in British Film
By Sarah Hill

girls like this, boys like that

---

the reproduction of gender in contemporary youth cultures

VICTORIA CANN

I.B. TAURIS
LONDON • NEW YORK • OXFORD • NEW DELHI • SYDNEY

I.B. TAURIS
Bloomsbury Publishing Plc
50 Bedford Square, London, WC1B 3DP, UK
1385 Broadway, New York, NY 10018, USA

BLOOMSBURY, I.B. TAURIS and the I.B. Tauris logo
are trademarks of Bloomsbury Publishing Plc

First published in Great Britain 2018
Paperback edition first published 2020

Copyright © Victoria Cann, 2018

Victoria Cann has asserted her right under the Copyright,
Designs and Patents Act, 1988, to be identified as Author of this work.

For legal purposes the Acknowledgements on p. xvii constitute
an extension of this copyright page.

All rights reserved. No part of this publication may be reproduced or
transmitted in any form or by any means, electronic or mechanical,
including photocopying, recording, or any information storage or retrieval
system, without prior permission in writing from the publishers.

Bloomsbury Publishing Plc does not have any control over, or responsibility for,
any third-party websites referred to or in this book. All internet addresses given
in this book were correct at the time of going to press. The author and publisher
regret any inconvenience caused if addresses have changed or sites have
ceased to exist, but can accept no responsibility for any such changes.

A catalogue record for this book is available from the British Library.

A catalog record for this book is available from the Library of Congress.

ISBN: HB: 978-1-7845-3564-3
PB: 978-1-3501-4436-1
ePDF: 978-1-8386-0862-0
eBook: 978-1-8386-0861-3

Series: Library of Gender and Popular Culture, volume 12

Typeset in Minion Pro by OKS Prepress Services, Chennai, India

To find out more about our authors and books visit
www.bloomsbury.com and sign up for our newsletters.

For Nanny, Mum and Alexia.
Excellent women; past, present and future

Contents

List of Illustrations	xiii
Series Editors' Foreword	xv
Acknowledgements	xvii
Introduction	**1**
Regulation at School	2
Challenges of Understanding Gender in Youth Taste Cultures	3
Taste Cultures as Regulatory	4
Theories of Contemporary Taste Cultures	6
Book Structure	8
1 Researching Youth Taste Cultures: The Study	**11**
Methodological Reflections and Considerations	12
The Schools	13
The Norfolk Context	15
The Research Process	16
Exploratory Ethnography	16
Identity Pages	18
Focus Groups	23
Conducting the Focus Groups	24
Identity Page Prompts	27
Television Listings Exercise	29
Matching-Up Exercise	32
Looking Forward: Designing Research Methodologies for Youth Taste Culture Research	33
2 Fitting in at School: The Context of Youth Taste Cultures	**35**
Appropriateness in Contemporary Youth Taste Culture	36
Regulating Taste at High School	38

Girls Like This, Boys Like That

Findings		38
School as Hyper-Regulatory		39
'Shunned': The Consequences of Inappropriate Articulations		42
Fitting into What?		44
Strategies of 'Fitting In'		46
Not Fitting In		51
Concluding Remarks		53

3 What is Gender? Theorising Gender and Young People's Lived Experiences — 55

Conceptualising Identity	55
(Re)producing Gender	57
Queering Gender	58
Gender as Performance: Performing Gender	59
'I Needed a Gay': Young People's Conceptualisations of Gender	61
Gender in Norfolk: Geographically Situating Gender	62
The Sex/Gender Distinction	63
The Persistence of the Gender Binary and its Knowability	68
Conflating Sexuality with Gender	69
Concluding Remarks	71

4 Boys Like This: Masculinity and Appropriate Tastes for Boys — 73

Theorising Masculinity and Boyhood(s): The Background	74
Hegemonic Masculinity Theory	75
Inclusive Masculinity Theory	76
Theorising and Understanding Boy Cultures: What We Know	78
Boys' Tastes, Masculinity and the Identity Pages	81
Masculine Value	82
Boys Like: Texts that Foreground Physicality	83
Boys Like: Violence, Conflict and Action	83

Contents

Boys Like: Sport	86
Boys Like: Music with Instruments	89
Boys Like: Sexy Girls	91
Concluding Remarks	94

5 Girls Like That: Femininity and Appropriate Tastes for Girls — 97
- Theorising Girlhood and Femininity: The Background — 99
- Femininities — 100
- The Complexities of Femininity in Lived Realities — 102
- Girls' Tastes, Femininity and the Identity Pages — 103
- Feminine Value — 104
- Girls Like: Romance — 106
- Girls Like: Singing and the Singers — 110
- Girls' Tastes and the (Re)Production of Gender Through Articulation: The Feminine Value of Bitching — 113
- Concluding Remarks — 117

6 Living on the Edge: Regulating and Transgressing Gender Appropriate Taste — 119
- Gender Appropriate Tastes — 121
- Boys and Gender Inappropriate Taste — 122
- Too Little Masculinity: Responses to Prompt Five — 123
- Too Much Masculinity: Responses to Prompt Three — 126
- Little Resistances? — 129
- Girls and Gender Inappropriate Taste — 132
- Little Resistances? — 134
- Troubling? — 137
- Fangirling as Resistance? — 137
- Concluding Remarks — 138

Conclusions and Recommendations — 141
- Youth Taste Cultures and Hyper-Regulation — 142
- Hyper-Regulation — 144
- Taste and the (Re)Production of Gender — 144

Reflections and Future Research 148
Reifying the Gender Binary? 150
Potential for Change? Recommendations and
   Cultural Sensitivities 151
Final Remarks 153

Notes 155
Bibliography 159
Index 169

List of Illustrations

Figures

Figure 1.1 School participation in data collection in the Norfolk region	14
Figure 1.2 Personality image	20
Figure 1.3 Blank identity page	21
Figure 1.4 Partially completed identity page	22
Figure 1.5 Prompt 2	28
Figure 1.6 TV listings exercise prompt example. Credit: Time Inc. for *What's On TV*	30
Figure 1.7 Exercise worksheet example – participant names redacted	31
Figure 2.1 Exercise worksheet example – participant names redacted	52
Figure 6.1 Prompt 5	123
Figure 6.2 Prompt 3	127
Figure 6.3 Prompt 8	135

Tables

Table 1.1 Participants' schools and sessions attended	25
Table 1.2 Focus group activities undertaken with each group, Group One, City High	26
Table 1.3 Focus group activities undertaken with each group, Group Two, City High	26

Table 1.4 Focus group activities undertaken with each group, Outskirts High 27

Table 1.5 Focus group activities undertaken with each group, Girls High 27

All images created by author unless otherwise specified.

Series Editors' Foreword

Gender in the school environment has long been a topic for academic study. Here, Victoria Cann poses the question: how do young people (re)produce gender and what role does taste in popular culture play in this process? She explores what gender means to young people and investigates the commonly held twenty-first-century belief that gender is a fluid concept for young people. She acknowledges that gendered stereotypes are both problematic and arbitrary, but her study suggests that they are nevertheless discursively powerful and we should acknowledge this as they play an important cultural role in the lives of young people.

Given that gender as a separate unit of analysis is so problematised through Bourdieu's understanding of distinction, Cann argues we need to look beyond the work of Bourdieu in our understanding of taste cultures. Because gendered distinctions lead to persistent inequalities at the level of gender (especially for ciswomen, trans and queer folk), asking questions and developing understanding of how these distinctions are normalised in everyday cultural practice is vital. In order to do this, Cann suggests, what is required is a much broader understanding of contemporary taste cultures.

Cann conceives of gender as beyond the body, understanding it as discursively (re)produced. Through this, she shows how these discourses of gender are (re)produced when young people talk about the things that they like and dislike; their taste cultures. Through interviews, focus groups, and data collected from an app, Cann's study explores the lives and popular culture tastes of a selection of young people (aged 13–16) in the small English city of Norwich. In so doing, many of the popular cultural texts that appear in monographs in other books in this Library can be seen afresh through the eyes of young consumers. As a means of understanding contemporary youth taste cultures, this study places young people's lived experiences at its heart, with methods designed specifically around their interests. The core age of participants in Cann's study was around 14 years old. By engaging with young people directly, she has been able to develop an invaluable understanding of their taste cultures as well as the ways in which gender is (re)produced within and through them. Their own words and activities illuminate Cann's discussion.

The context for the majority of this research is based in the school environment. Cann shows that gender appropriate taste matters because high school can be considered a 'hyper-regulatory space', and so young people are motivated to articulate appropriately so as not to be ostracised. Her participants routinely discursively devalued femininity, with many young people distancing themselves from it. In addition, there are also clear distinctions between femininity and masculinity. Such findings are important because they reveal the persistence of gender divisions during youth. The relevance of this to the wider Library are clear, no more so than in the pseudonyms the young participants choose for themselves. As Cann's discussion of these shows, these names can tell us a lot about the relevance of popular cultural taste to this age group.

What this study shows, is that popular culture plays an important part in the ways in which boys and girls deploy taste to fit in, or to not fit in. As Cann argues, there is a persistence in terms of binary gender divisions. She acknowledges that queer and non-binary youth are highly visible in popular culture in the UK, but that in reality, such young people must be very brave due to their very existence challenging the dominant gender discourses in the hyper-regulatory context of high school. The cultural tastes of the participants in Cann's study reflect the expectations of narrowly-defined genders, with little scope for divergent sexuality to be constructed.

Cann shows that school can be a hyper-regulatory space, and because young people fear being shunned, they have the motivation to articulate appropriate taste. Her book therefore finishes with a section that offers suggestions for how her research can be used in policy formation.

– Angela Smith and Claire Nally

Acknowledgements

I knew that writing this book would be difficult, I was somewhat prepared for that. But writing the acknowledgements, this is hard. This book comes out of my PhD and so there were four years of writing that and then there were the post-doc years where the time to turn this into a book became a squeeze. All in all I've been researching and writing this book for about eight years, there will undoubtedly people who I don't mention by name that I couldn't have done this without. Please know that I appreciate you.

Eight years is a long time, so much of my personal life has changed (the beginning, middle and end of relationships, loss of loved ones, mental breakdowns as well as some good stuff) and so to those around who have loved and supported and picked up the pieces, this book would not have happened without you. So thank you to my Mum, my sisters (Dionne and Katherine), Jodie Paget ('one of my best friends'), Erica Horton (also survived), Charlene Katuwawala and Joe Naylor, Georgia Walker Churchman, Ashleyanne Krigbaum, Jo Beckett-King, Jess Ludlow, Kate and Jem Eaves, Stina Odeen-Isbister, Helen Warner and Walter and Abraham.

This book is dedicated to my family, my Nanny who never got to hold the final copy of my thesis but who means so much and is the reason I am here at all. My wonderful Mum, my sisters, my Uncle Tony, my niece Alexia, my cousins and my aunts and uncles. And to my Dad, who I wish I could have known. You all are my everything.

To my friends at the University of East Anglia, Helen Warner, Sarah Godfrey, my mentor Yvonne Tasker, Sanna Inthorn and John Street (without whom none of this would have been a possibility). To the Faculty of Arts and Humanities for funding my research and helping me get this book past the finish line. I especially want to thank the wonderful folks in the Interdisciplinary Institute for the Humanities who are much more than just 'colleagues'. I am very lucky to be a part of this department, special thanks to Liz Powell and Francisco Costa. And of course to Tom Phillips who has made me laugh more times than I can count.

Girls Like This, Boys Like That

To Heather Savigny and Sarah Powell for their endless and inexplicable pride. You are both motivating and inspiring. To the students that I have taught over the past nine years, especially that handful who really get lit up by feminist theory, you have sustained me to keep writing. To the schools and the participants that took part in this study, thank you, please keep opening your doors to us researchers, we value your openness more than you can imagine. To the people I have met at conferences and seminars and workshops, and my academic network on Twitter, you make academia an exciting and hopeful place to be in what are difficult times. Here's to more collaboration and fewer dickheads.

To my kind and patient editors at I.B.Tauris, Anna Coatman who started the process and Lisa Goodrum who finished it (that's how long it took) and to Arub Ahmed who actually turned it into a book. Tam Sanger for copyediting (you had your work cut out) and Naya Clark for indexing, thank you. Emma Belka, you are a wonderful artist.

Ryan Hillier, you played such an important role in my life during this process, I want to acknowledge that here.

Finally, thanks to the #ResSisters for everything (#shinebright). May we all find our collectives to challenge sexism, racism, homophobia, ableism, ageism and neoliberal imperatives in our lives and the lives of others. We always stand stronger together and in solidarity. There is more power in people than people in power.

Finally, I would like to thank Beyoncé for writing Lemonade.

And Helen Warner, have I mentioned her? She really is a babe.

Oh, and my therapist of course, I really should thank her too.

Introduction

Mary: A bit sad really, that boys all have to like one thing and girls all like another
Sara: Well they don't have to
Mary: Yeah, but they'd get laughed at if they didn't!
(City High, Session One, Group Two)

In the above excerpt from one of the focus groups that I ran with groups of British teenagers, Mary and Sara reflect on the regulatory role of taste. From Facebook pages and dating profiles to everyday conversations, much of our lives are bound up in discussion of the things we like and dislike; our tastes say so much about who we are. But, of course, it is much more complicated than that. Conversations at dinner can become fraught when I discuss with my sister, a fan of MotoGP rider Valentino Rossi, how much I like the rider Jorge Lorenzo. My students' discussions of what is or isn't cool instantly make me feel naff and out of touch. And then there are our 'guilty pleasures' that only a select few get to know about (in my case think Ricky Martin, *Keeping up with the Kardashians*, and pretty much any made-for-TV movie ever produced). We self-censor in our conversations and we judge others for their tastes; we are complicit in the reproduction of 'appropriate' taste. Taste is everywhere and taste *matters*.

Let's think about the cultural worlds of young people for a moment. In a time when gender is supposed to be more fluid than ever we have seen a resurgence of the gender binary. All I need to do is try to buy a 'gender-neutral' gift for my six-year-old niece to experience the stubborn persistence of gender and its limitations. Lego, perhaps formerly the most gender-neutral toy of our time, has gone 'pink'. Ignore (if we can) for a moment the racialised whiteness of figures and consider what possibilities are now available to our generation of tomorrow in the worlds of such toys.

The introduction of the Lego Friends range in 2012 brought with it the idea that construction was for boys and figurine play for girls. Rather than simply free building, the Friends range encourages girls to spend less time building spaces and more time playing with the characters in their worlds. Perhaps even more concerning are some of the sets available in this range, including for example a Pop Star Dressing Room, a Cupcake Café, and a Pet Salon. But of course this is not a book about the pinkification of culture (there are lots of good ones already out there on this topic: Orenstein (2012), Hains (2012) and so forth), it is a book about how young people like Mary and Sara above experience their cultural worlds as gendered.

Regulation at School

My mum has spent much of her working life as a dinner lady at a primary school in Norfolk and often tells me of the 'playground politics' she witnesses on a daily basis. Boys quickly learn that coming to school with their nails painted is not acceptable behaviour for anyone other than girls; meanwhile girls learn that wearing the 'right' items of clothing should be their primary concern. Such politics of gender appropriate behaviour limits who and what these young people can be – they shrink their future possibilities and worlds. There are clear rules about what is gender appropriate and what is not, and in this book I show that this is no more acutely felt than at high school during the period of youth.

There is much anxiety surrounding the lives of British youth; self-harm remains a growing and pernicious element of youth culture, with reports indicating that the UK has had the highest rate of self-harm in Europe (Horrocks, House and Owens 2002). When we introduce gender into the frame it becomes even more concerning. As Barker (2005) writes, boys are dying to become men and countless critics, including Politician Diane Abbott (2013), have lamented the 'crisis of masculinity' facing British boys (see Roberts 2014). Girls meanwhile are killing themselves in the quest to look skinny (Holmes 2017) and finding themselves the subject of continued sexual abuse on the streets (Bates 2014). When we think outside of the gender binary things are arguably even worse, with trans-youth killing themselves (when not being killed) to be accepted (Grossman and D'Augelli 2007). Through social networking sites such as Facebook, Instagram and Snapchat, young people's lives are open to observation and

Introduction

comment 24 hours a day. Young people are facing challenges that are wholly different to those faced by the generations before them, and never before has the careful negotiation of self-presentation been such a permeating affair.

Challenges of Understanding Gender in Youth Taste Cultures

The main question behind this book is: how do young people (re)produce gender and what role does taste play in this process? In this research I explore what gender means to young people and find that gender is a somewhat stable category for them. Gender is understood in relation to (but not defined by) the sexed body, which young people in this study see as operating in a binary form (ultimately one is either male *or* female from this perspective). In this book I conceive of gender as *beyond* the body, understanding it as discursively (re)produced. More specifically I am interested in how these discourses of gender are (re)produced when young people talk about the things that they like and dislike; their taste cultures.

If you take the same position as me, that gender exists beyond the body and is therefore discursively produced and not an essentially existing category, then it makes asking questions of how gender is (re)produced somewhat tricky. It is difficult because if we accept that the body does not make gender but rather discourse does, then we are nevertheless left with the challenge of categorising different behaviours/tastes/texts as 'gendered'. This is problematic as through categorisation we run the risk of 'stereotyping and/or reify[ing] gender binaries' (Francis 2010a: 478). I respond to this issue in this work by conceiving of gender as something that is inscribed by people in relation to 'the masculine' and 'the feminine', which is associated with the 'behaviours of boys' and the 'behaviours of girls'. I discuss the idea that gender is something that young people inscribe based on the understanding that (for them) there *is* a gender binary and that gendered stereotypes (and/or expectations) help them to make sense of this (even if they do not always agree with the stereotypes, as the empirical chapters show).

I am not arguing that these inscriptions are inherent or 'natural', but rather aim to deconstruct them so that we can better understand how gender is (re)produced. This is important because if we can learn how young people (re)produce gender then we can learn how to best intervene, because, as I have illustrated above, through the (re)production of gender the possibilities of who and what young people can be remain limited. Thus, while we might want to abandon such stereotypes, as they are both problematic and arbitrary, they are nevertheless discursively powerful and we should acknowledge this as they play an important cultural role in the lives of young people.

Existing academic literature indicates that by exploring youth in particular, we may be able to glimpse transgression and change, as it has been argued that 'young people can tell us a lot about the scale and dynamics of social change' (McRobbie 1994: 179). In understanding gender to be arbitrary, youth becomes an interesting site through which to think about the (re)production of gender, as youth is considered to be 'one of the most likely sites where prevailing ideas about identity and status are questioned, suspended or reversed' (Hesmondhalgh 2005: 37). However, given the persistence of the gender binary, I am not so sure that youth provides a *de facto* space for change and transgression. Part of this belief results from the understanding that 'gender is not simply a matter of choice, but a negotiation that occurs within a matrix of social and historical forces' (Nayak and Kehily 2008: 5). Gender is a crucial site of academic interrogation because 'it may open doors in our lives, limit or broaden our possibilities to live our lives to the fullest' (Järviluoma, Moisala and Vilkko 2003: 6); gender continues to limit who and what we can be. Developing an understanding of how these discourses are (re)produced and the ways in which they regulate us can therefore allow us to see how this unequal distribution of power is sustained within contemporary youth cultures and beyond.

Taste Cultures as Regulatory

Gans conceives of tastes as cultural forms that express values (1974: 10), and I narrow this definition to one that focuses on the collective cultures of judgement that pertain to cultural texts. In this definition I think about how judgement is collectively produced, and thus I understand taste to be wholly social, something that only has meaning when it is expressed (articulated) and comprehended. Because taste is worked out *collectively*,

Introduction

a shared sense of what taste positions are appropriate and why is developed – this can help us to see how gender is both understood and (re)produced in relation to these discourses. I am therefore interested in how value orientations are worked out in relation to dominant taste cultures. As such, I do not think of taste in terms of 'good' or 'bad', but rather I ask 'what is acceptable?', 'what is appropriate?' and 'what discourses produce this subjectivity?' By thinking about articulations of judgement in terms of acceptability we are able to think about taste not as innate, but as culturally negotiated. In doing so a number of questions are raised, such as: 'what judgements are articulated and why?' and 'what might be the consequence of inappropriate taste?' These questions begin to be answered in the empirical chapters of this book (Chapters 4–6).

Veblen's (1899) theories of conspicuous consumption, developed at the turn of the last century, demonstrate the long history of academic interrogation into taste cultures. However, it is only in the wake of Pierre Bourdieu's conceptual developments in the academic field that taste has been understood as playing a role in the (re)production of identity. Bourdieu has had a profound influence on how academics have thought about taste, forcing us to consider the ways in which 'taste classifies, and it classifies the classifier' (2010: xxix). Importantly, Bourdieu has helped us to appreciate the relationship between taste and power, asking questions about how 'tastes arise out of, and are mobilised in, struggles for social power' (Jenkins 2002: 129). In terms of taste cultures more specifically, Bourdieu's conceptualisation of different forms of capital (cultural, economic and social) can aid in our understanding of how power is reproduced, because it is in the distribution of these capitals that we are able to identify 'micropolitics of power' (Skeggs 1997: 8).

Cultural capital (knowing the 'right' things) gives individuals a means of distinguishing themselves from one another in terms of their cultural tastes. This leads to particular groups defining their taste cultures as superior to those of other groups (Bennett et al. 2009), such that legitimacy can be enjoyed (Prieur and Savage 2011: 577). As Pedrozo writes, 'people take advantage of consumption practices to reproduce, raise or reinforce their social status in a symbolic way' (2011: 116). These ideas surrounding legitimacy, status and superior tastes are strengths offered by Bourdieu's theories when it comes to class, but are complicated when applied to gender. This is because when striving to achieve legitimacy in relation to dominant discourses of gender, the investment in cultural texts that are understood as either 'appropriate' or 'inappropriate' does not necessarily confer privilege in terms of value or advantage. This is to say that if 'cultural capital works rather like property [whereby] those with it gain at the expense from those without' (Bennett et al. 2009: 11), it may be hard to imagine how one could gain by being *more* feminine or *more* masculine. This is especially true because femininity occupies a lower cultural position to masculinity under patriarchy, and masculinity has been arguably understood as increasingly inclusive (see Anderson 2009; McCormack 2012). Thus, if metaphors of capital are to help us understand symbolic wealth in society (Huppatz 2009: 45) we can see that masculinity remains 'wealthy' under patriarchy. However, the value of femininity is much more complex as it is an 'amalgam of practice and appearance, it can be simultaneously negative and positive' (Skeggs 2004a: 27). This is not to say that the values of masculinity are not complex, but rather that under patriarchy the value of femininity is negotiated in different ways. This focus on gender and its nuances with respect to taste reminds us of a wider absence of gender within Bourdieu's original concept of cultural capital.[1]

Given that gender as a separate unit of analysis is so problematised through Bourdieu's understanding of distinction, we need to look beyond the work of Bourdieu in our understanding of taste cultures. Because gendered distinctions lead to persistent inequalities at the level of gender (especially for ciswomen, trans and queer folk[2]), asking questions and developing understanding of *how* these distinctions are normalised in everyday cultural practice is vital. What is required then is a much broader understanding of contemporary taste cultures.

Theories of Contemporary Taste Cultures

In recent years a more flexible understanding of contemporary taste cultures has emerged through thinking outside of Bourdieu's somewhat (structurally) restrictive framework. Other studies in this field have focused on the concept of omnivorousness, incorporating an appreciation of the breadth of tastes.

Bethany Bryson has provided an invaluable contribution to the academic field by urging us to think not only of cultural *preferences*, but

Introduction

also *negative* cultural evaluations (1996: 884). In doing so she reminds us of the importance of relationality within taste cultures. Taste is a basis of social exclusion and so we need to examine what is *not* liked as well as what *is* in order to understand the full story of taste. Bryson (1996, 1997) explicates social exclusion through taste, arguing that taste can tell us much about the subtle forces of power that are at work. Discussion of tastes and cultural consumption can therefore provide sites where some individuals and groups are 'Othered'. However, to suggest or assume that taste cultures are a neat and organised set of responses to cultural texts would be to overlook the complexities of consumption in contemporary culture. For example, Karvonen et al. have argued that 'established sets of values are becoming increasingly fragmented, suggesting it is increasingly popular to have dissonant, even conflicting values' (2012: 34). This demonstrates clear shifts in taste cultures from the time that Bourdieu was writing, complicating our understanding of how taste cultures operate, and thereby requiring further academic interrogation to be undertaken.

Taste culture research is a rich and diverse field, yet despite this youth and gender remain vastly underexplored within it. The period of youth offers an important context in the development of understanding gender (re)production through taste. In the first instance, youth is considered to offer a glimpse of the 'new adulthood' and thus through the examination of youth we can start to imagine what gender might look like in the future (Nayak and Kehily 2006; White and Wyn 2004). Furthermore, there are conflicting accounts of how regulatory the period of youth actually is, with some approaches indicating that it is a period of discursive transgression and creativity (Hesmondhalgh 2005; McRobbie 1994) and others, looking at gender more specifically, understanding it to be a period of considerable regulation (Epstein and Johnson 1998; Frosh, Phoenix and Pattman 2002; Rasmussen 2004).

As a means of understanding contemporary youth taste cultures, this study places young people's lived experiences at its heart, with methods designed specifically around their interests. In total I engaged with 112 people from the Norfolk region, which is in the east of England, with a further 28 participants taking part in an exploratory ethnography. The core age of participants was around 14 years old. By engaging with young people directly I have been able to develop an invaluable understanding of their taste cultures as well as the ways in which gender is (re)produced within and through them. I illuminate their experiences throughout this book, often with reference to their own words and activities.

Book Structure

In this work I explore the complex world of contemporary youth taste cultures by examining the broad academic fields of taste and gender studies. In Chapter 1, 'Researching Youth Taste Cultures', I provide an overview of the sample and methods employed within this research, discussing the context of the young people that took part in this study, as well as reflecting on my approach to some of the challenges I faced in the course of my research. I draw on my own experiences of undertaking empirical audience studies research to show the usefulness of a qualitative approach in audience studies, as well as emphasising the need to account for complexities of meaning in the interrogation of taste.

The case for undertaking research into contemporary youth taste cultures is made in Chapter 2, 'Fitting in at School'. It is here that I present empirical research alongside theoretical works to show the regulation of gender that takes place in high school. As part of this discussion I make the case that high school in the UK is a 'hyper-regulatory' space, as a result of the amount of time that young people spend together on school grounds. I show in this chapter some of the regulatory consequences of making 'inappropriate' taste articulations, with the majority of young people fearing being 'shunned'. The consequences of this in terms of gender are elucidated in Chapters 4, 5 and 6 of the book.

The book progresses, in Chapter 3, by considering the ways in which young people conceptualise gender, with their perspectives located within the context of the academic field. I demonstrate that while young people are willing to consider and accept more fluid ideas of gender, they remain somewhat wedded to ideas of a knowable and discoverable gender identity that exists within the gender binary. Within this chapter I therefore highlight the disjuncture between the progressions in the academic field of queer theory, and the experiences of young people living today.

Introduction

The book then uses the understanding and context built in the previous chapters to examine in greater depth the (re)production of gender in contemporary youth taste cultures. These empirically focused chapters are structured in a way that acknowledges the unfixedness of gender, but it has been necessarily fixed onto the pages as a means of coherently working through the young people's experiences of gender and gendered expectations. As part of this I explore what is valued in terms of masculinity and femininity, I work through different taste articulations, and consider how and/or why participants see particular articulations as being gender (in)appropriate. I think about the experiences of young people such as Mary and Sara whose words opened this chapter. Such reflections allow me to illustrate just how differently taste is experienced by boys and girls, as well as some of the regulatory consequences of some taste articulations. For example, in Chapter 4, 'Boys Like This', I think about taste that is considered appropriate for 'boys' (that is, individuals who have been attributed a youth male identity) alongside the (re)production of masculinity. By looking at what people of a particular gender are imagined to like we can start to think about the inscription of gender into cultural texts and tastes. I then focus on girls' tastes in Chapter 5, 'Girls Like That', and how we can think about this in relation to femininity. I find that what is appropriate for girls is much broader than what is appropriate for boys, showing that taste cultures are experienced differently by those who present as girls and those who present as boys. I then explore in Chapter 6, 'Living on the Edge', whether or not we can see any transgressions of gender in taste articulation, showing the highly nuanced ways in which discourses of gender are employed to rein-in potentially problematic tastes.

In the 'Conclusion and Recommendations' I discuss how through this rich and innovative study I have found that taste *does* matter in contemporary youth taste cultures and that gender is discursively (re)produced when taste is articulated. I argue that 'appropriate' articulations of taste (re)produce dominant gender discourses. Gender-appropriate taste matters because high school is what I consider a 'hyper-regulatory space', and so young people are motivated to articulate appropriately so as not to be ostracised. Femininity was routinely discursively de-valued with many young people distancing themselves from it, and I also found clear distinctions between femininity and masculinity. Such findings are important because they reveal the persistence of gender divisions during youth. Taste cultures may appear trivial and inconsequential, but I reveal in this research that they are not innocuous; regulating and limiting the parameters of who and what young people can be in terms of gender. To respond to these findings I therefore set out meaningful ways in which changes can be achieved in contemporary society and culture.

1

Researching Youth Taste Cultures: The Study

When I started this research I wanted young people's voices to be at the foreground of my study, and so an underlying principle has been to ensure that the findings and development of methods have been informed directly by the experiences of young people. While the older among us reading this have been 14 years old at some point in our lives, our experiences will be highly distinct from those who are 14 now. Raced, classed and (dis)abled experiences will only further impact these experiences, memories and understandings. Stockton's work on the queerness of childhood highlights this tension well, when she writes, '[t]he child is simply who we are not, and in fact never were. It is the act of adults looking back' (2009: 5). Perhaps, as adults, we can never really *know* children.

Researching youth is, as with many other social groups, in many ways bound up in power relations. As an academic researcher I cannot help but be older than my research subjects. In a country where people under the age of 16 have little autonomy, there remains what Ferguson calls an 'enormous chasm of power that separates grown-ups and young people' (2001: 13). Such power dynamics must be attended to when conducting research.

Methodological Reflections and Considerations

Researching youth gender subjectivities is tricky. It is tricky because identity is in its very nature subjective and during the transitional period of youth the parameters of acceptability are being worked out in a heightened manner. The methods that we use in our empirical research must therefore account for such complexities, whilst also attending to ethical considerations. Thus through the combination of the three methods used in this study we can begin to account for the plurality of youth experiences (as argued by McRobbie 1994) and the emphasis on meaning in qualitative research can help to capture this.

The combination of methods used throughout this research study is intended to delve further under the surface. Through my use of ethnography, identity pages and focus groups I have attended to the cultures of everyday life, with the aim of capturing an understanding of the lived experiences of young people. When researching youth and gender there is also a need to consider the ways in which research plays an ideological role, both in reproducing academic common sense about young people (Griffin 1993: 2) and about gender (Järviluoma, Moisala and Vilkko 2003: 18–20). The ethics of our research therefore extends beyond the treatment and care of our research subjects and ourselves, as it is also bound up in the construction of knowledge. All of the methods detailed below have been designed with the research subjects in mind, but beyond the design framework there remains a need for researchers to engage in practices of reflexivity.

One of the ways in which reflexivity can be achieved is by recognising our role as researchers, and in particular the impact that our social and cultural backgrounds have on our research. This has a dual importance in research engaging with youth, as we are forced to attend to both our position as adults in a power relationship with the young people of our studies, and to the role that memory plays in our understanding of youth. As a white (cis)female, working-class woman I occupy a number of positions of power. Consideration of, and reflection upon, the 'plethora of power struggles' (Dunbar, Rodriguez and Parker, 2001: 281) and the impact that these identities of mine have on my research subjects – particularly those of colour – is worthy of serious consideration.

In terms of memory and geography, occupying a reflexive position allows one to minimise the influence their own memories have on the reading of the participants' experiences. For example, growing up in Norwich (the city of study) brings with it both strengths and weaknesses. I have a rich and in-depth understanding of the area and knowledge of the places that participants talk about. However, I have also engaged, and continue to engage, with the spaces in very different ways to the participants of my study. I either view these spaces in relation to the past, and thus through memory, or with respect to the present but as an adult. As Thorne has argued, memory is both an 'obstacle and resource in the process of doing work with kids' (1993: 7). I therefore follow the work of Biklen who writes that researchers need to 'name and interrogate' our memories in carrying out research with young people (2004: 724).

What I aim to show in this chapter is that there are issues we need to confront when undertaking research with young people, but that there are ways in which in which we can grapple with them and produce meaningful understandings in the process. I outline here the three methods that I employed in this research – ethnography, online identity pages and focus groups – and explore the knowledge that I have built through the use of these methods, outlining the ways in which they can be employed in future taste culture and youth culture research. As part of this process I raise wider epistemological questions of doing feminist research to answer questions related to youth experience.

The Schools

The schools that took part in this study were selected based on their geographical location within Norfolk and their willingness to take part in the study. Given the increasing pressure and time constraints that teachers face within the British education system, my choices of where this research could be undertaken were governed largely by the availability of the schools. I have anonymised the names of the schools in line with the promises made to the participants and their parents/guardians. I have included contextual information below so as to better understand the background of the data collection sites, but much has been generalised so as not to disclose identities.

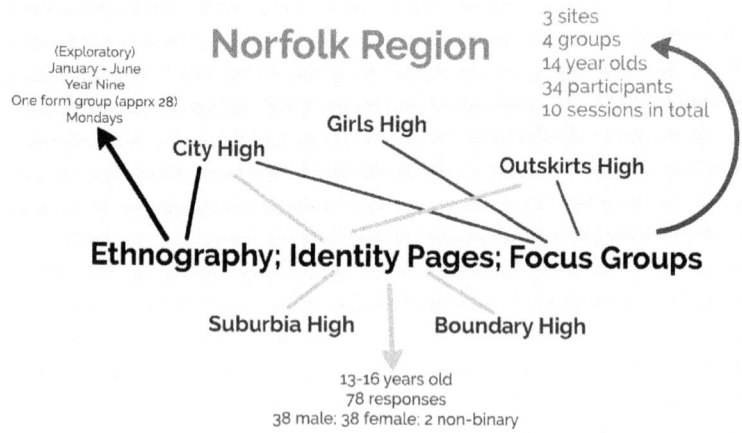

Figure 1.1 School participation in data collection in the Norfolk region

Boundary High

Boundary High is a co-ed comprehensive with under 1,000 students from a low socio-economic background located in proximity to a city in Norfolk. The proportion of students receiving the pupil premium[1] during the period of data collection was above the national average. The school is more ethnically diverse than other schools in the region but is lower than the national average. However, the number of pupils who speak English as an additional language is closer to the national average.

City High

City High is a co-ed comprehensive with under 1,000 students from a low socio-economic background located in close proximity to a city in Norfolk. At the time of data collection, the proportion of students that received the pupil premium was above the national average and the majority of students that attended the school are White-British.

Girls High

Girls High is an independent school in Norfolk that has under 1,000 students, all of whom are female. Students are largely from an affluent background and the majority of its students are White-British.

Outskirts High

Outskirts High is a large co-ed comprehensive with over 1,000 students from a predominantly low socio-economic background located in the outskirts of a Norfolk city. The school site is split into two (they do not mix until they are placed into 'sets' for their GCSEs), and I have called each half of the split 'East Side' and 'West Side'. The proportion of students who received the pupil premium during the period of data collection was below the national average and the majority of students that attend this school are White-British.

Suburbia High

Suburbia High is a co-ed comprehensive with over 1,000 students that largely come from a relatively middle class socio-economic background and it is located in close proximity to a Norfolk city. The number of students eligible for the pupil premium at the time of data collection was below the national average and the majority of students are White-British.

The Norfolk Context

All of the data was collected in the proximity of a city in Norfolk, which is significant. This city, the only in the county, Norwich, is marked by its isolation, with few major roads servicing the area (there are no motorways) and transport connections to other major cities and counties being relatively poor.

Poor transport links and its location within the east of England mean that, despite having a relatively large population (there are over 200,000 residents), the city remains somewhat isolated in relation to the rest of the country. However, as with the participants of Vanderbeck and Dunkley's (2003) study, the position of the city in a rural area means that while many outsiders may view the general location as rural, this is more complicated for those living in its proximity. For residents of the nearby villages, the coastal towns of Norfolk and Suffolk, as well as the in-land market towns, Norwich can often be viewed as more of a metropolis in relation to its surroundings. In this way then, Norwich is an interesting place as it straddles the rural and the urban – complicating binary conceptions of young people as either urban *or* rural (see Hopkins 2010: 239). As I demonstrate in Chapter 3, the rurality or 'backwardness' of Norfolk was also considered significant to the participants and their lived socio-cultural experiences.

The Research Process

When I was a teenager I was a bit of a nightmare. I cared a lot about doing well at school (that was the competitive side of me) but I was also outspoken, I swore a lot and questioned the power of everyone around me. Teachers that liked me would describe me as 'high energy', while teachers that did not would describe me as 'bolshy'. As an adult, in many ways young people frighten me because the young version of me kind of scared me – what if the teens I met were like I was? I questioned whether I was the right person to do this research. I figured the best thing I could do was rip off the Band-Aid and engage in youth culture from the outset, letting the young people guide my research design, leading to the first of the three methods that I used in this research – the exploratory ethnography.

Exploratory Ethnography

Drawing on my commitment to feminist research methods and my desire to immerse myself in the world of young people, there seemed to be much sense in undertaking an ethnography. By doing this in the early stages of my research I was able to develop a firsthand understanding of contemporary youth culture(s), providing an invaluable context for the development of the methods that followed it. This is because ethnographies involve 'getting close' and 'becoming part of the natural setting' (Fielding 1993: 156–7). Observing young people in the school setting allowed me to discover their interests and thoughts about particular topics, as well as how they engage with one another in a social context.

Observational methods have been relatively common within the context of British youth studies, due in part to Paul Willis' seminal work,

Learning to Labour, published in 1978. The fact that Willis used a school-based longitudinal ethnography has been emphasised as the reason he was able to get his research subjects, 'the lads', to open up, allowing him to achieve what he termed a far greater depth of understanding than other methods may have allowed (1978: 5). Arguably due to Willis' success in capturing the complexities of the gendered and classed youth experience, a number of other academics within the British and Irish context have undertaken ethnographies within school environments (Blackman 1998; Ging 2005; Hey 2002; Nayak and Kehily 2008). While I have found that the ethnography was somewhat limited in its practical ability to answer my research questions about how gender is (re)produced in taste articulation, it did provide a useful insight into the youth experience that helped to shape the research design that follows.

The ethnography took place within the first year of the project, commencing at the start of the 2011 Spring Term (January) and closing at the end of the 2011 Summer Term (July). Observations took place at City High (see school overview above) once a week during timetabled lessons, on the playground, in school hallways and during lunch breaks in the library. I recorded notes using a notepad and pen and spent most of my time watching rather than writing. Mondays were a particularly fruitful day of the week to conduct this type of research as it allowed me to hear the participants discussing the things that they had done over the weekend, including the films they had seen and the television they had watched, as well as other activities they had undertaken. Furthermore, the timetable on Mondays for this cohort was highly varied, including classes such as Art, Citizenship, Dance, Geography, History and Religious Studies. Observing students in lessons such as Art, Citizenship and Dance allowed me to gain a greater sense of young people's cultural practices.

The ethnography was an energising and motivating experience and gave me a far greater sense of young people's lives than reading any number of journal articles or books could do. Importantly too, it showed me that young people do regulate taste on the grounds of appropriateness and that discussion of culture, and in particular popular culture, was a central part of their lived experiences. To exemplify, in one lesson I heard a group of four boys discussing rock music, where one of them asked the other 'Mudhoney or Slipknot?' to which the boy carefully assessed the situation before responding 'Mudhoney' which was clearly the 'right' answer and the one that his peers were expecting from him. I witnessed groups of girls singing in the corridor and boys playing air guitar; I observed dance lessons where boys and girls opted to separate themselves almost entirely along gender lines, I saw some girls sit in silence running through their routine while some boys complained about the pop music the teacher was playing and not wanting to dance. In Art classes I saw students otherwise disengaged with school come to life around creative projects and in Citizenship classes I heard boys and girls employing essentialist accounts of the self in order to understand differences between genders.

While invigorating, the ethnography did also reveal to me some of the practical difficulties of answering research questions using purely observational methods. I found that when observing large groups of young people (such as the average of 30 pupils in a class at a British high school) it was difficult to focus on particular conversations between group members. This meant that I was forced to listen to those closest to me or those who were loudest, and thus in the collection of data this would mean that my findings would be disproportionately slanted towards those pupils who had the confidence to speak loudly, leading to a likely potential for marginalised groups to be underrepresented.

What I learned from the ethnography, in terms of my methods, was that I would need to think carefully about how I wanted to engage young people in the research process. On the whole they were reluctant to engage in practices that they could not clearly understand the purpose of. I knew that the largely quantitative survey/questionnaire approach that had dominated in previous taste studies research (see Bennett et al. 2009; Bourdieu 2010; Silva and Wright 2008) would not necessarily hold the attention of the young people I was looking to engage with. Such observations led directly to the development of online identity pages, to which I now turn.

Identity Pages

One of my enduring memories of young people's lives while undertaking observation at City High was the role that digital media technologies played in their lives. Seeing pupils with mobile telephones and MP3 players was a common occurrence and they often talked of the role that social media platforms such as Facebook played in their lives. Given the burgeoning field of apps for smartphones such as Instagram, Snapchat and Facebook, we can only assume that these social media outlets have become even more popular in the years since this research was conducted. Working with an educational technology specialist (Abi Evans) and web developer (Joe Naylor), I developed what I have called an 'Identity Page' which drew on these experiences and engaged with research participants in more engaging and playful ways.

Despite being 'vibrant exploding and developing' (Gauntlett 2000: 4), and thus having vast potential for cultural researchers seeking to engage in innovative research methods, the internet has so far been used primarily in the dissemination of questionnaires, surveys, netnographies or as a site for textual analysis (see Kozinets 2010). It is my contention that despite being nearly 20 years old, Slack's statement that 'we do not exploit the full potential of the medium' (1998: 1.3) continues to ring true. It is not my aim here to say that I *have* been able to meet the full potential of the internet – far from it – but I do hope that I have been able to encourage other researchers to consider its wider potential. Particularly given the permeance of apps, researchers would do well to work interdisciplinarily with computer and educational technologists to engage with social groups in cultural studies research and intervene in creative ways.

The identity pages that I developed were inspired by an art project I was given access to during my exploratory ethnography at City High, which involved young people creating a 'personality' image around a standardised framework provided by the teacher (a rudimentary version is displayed in Figure 1.2). This places the student's identity at the heart of the exercise, asking them to reflect on their cultural practices and to connect these practices and experiences to who they think they are. Most students became quickly engaged in the process, enjoying having the time to reflect on their identities.

In previous taste culture research, Silva and Wright reflected on their use of questionnaires, saying that they had 'reduced survey respondents to a series of clicks on a laptop mouse' (2008: 60). The identity page acts as a way of minimising this as it encourages respondents to immerse

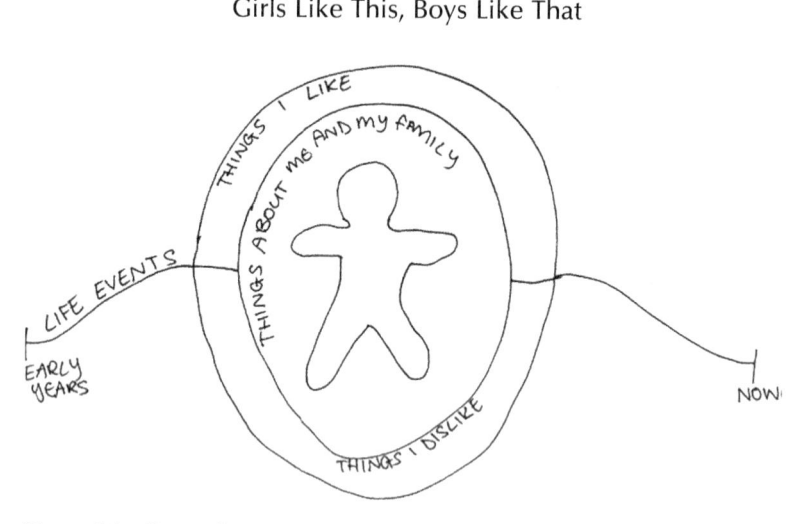

Figure 1.2 Personality image

themselves creatively in the production of their own identity page. Much as the pupils at City High did in their art classes, the identity pages were designed to empower participants so that they were able to use their own words as much as possible. To further connect themselves to the identity page process, the educational technologist and I developed an avatar that could be manipulated to resemble the participant in the centre of the screen (see Figures 1.3 and 1.4).

After liaising with teaching staff at a range of schools in Norfolk, explaining the research aims of the project and the content of the website, four schools from the region agreed to use the identity pages within timetabled lessons as well as to disseminate information so that pupils could complete them in their spare time. These schools were Boundary High, City High, Outskirts High, and Suburbia High, and the majority of identity pages were collected during school time, under the supervision of a member of teaching staff. The identity pages were collected in 2011 with respondents from across the High School cohort invited to take part (aged between 11–16, although I only received responses from those aged 13–16 years old). As the aim of the identity pages was to provide an understanding of young people's tastes I did not limit the sample to a particular cohort, nor did I rigidly constrain potential answers. Participants accessed the website by visiting a secure web address that was dedicated to this research project. The name of the website,

Researching Youth Taste Cultures

Part 2- More About Me

Next I would like you to describe some of your likes/dislikes and your appearance.

Television		Movies
😊 Television I like...		😊 Movies I like...
☹ Television I dislike...		☹ Movies I dislike...
Music		Websites
😊 Music I like...		😊 Websites I like...
☹ Music I dislike...		☹ Websites I dislike...
Celebrities		Other
😊 Celebrities I like...		😊 Other things I like...
☹ Celebrities I dislike...		☹ Other things I dislike...

Background color: ▢   submit

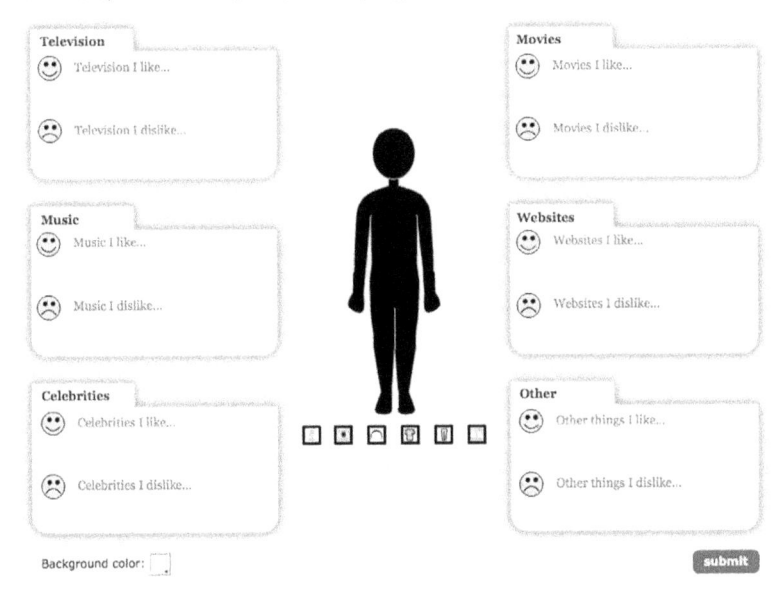

Figure 1.3 Blank identity page

'So This Is Me' (www.sothisisme.net – now defunct), was chosen to reflect its casualness, so that respondents did not feel pressure to perform a particularly 'serious' version of themselves that they may have associated with more formal surveys or titles.

Participants were able to construct their own versions of themselves, choosing the background from a spectrum of colours and filling in the boxes around the central avatar with their likes and dislikes. The aim was that by creating a version of themselves and changing the background colours they could inject the space with their own personality and thus connect themselves to the process. This was based on the understanding that, by seeing themselves on the screen, and especially through personalisation, users identify with the avatar that they create (Boberg, Piippo and Ollila 2008: 237). The activity was created to be as simple as possible, with easy click boxes so that as many respondents as possible could be involved. The setup of the identity pages and their adaptability is demonstrated in Figure 1.4.

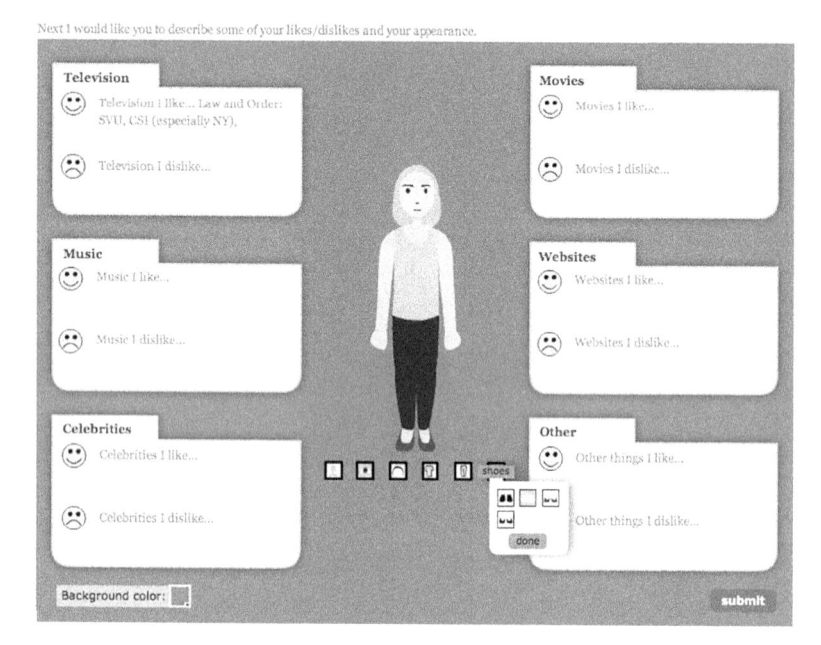

Figure 1.4 Partially completed identity page

As part of the process respondents who took part in the activity were able to change the background colours by selecting from the spectrum wheel, adapt the avatar to look like themselves and fill in the blanks using their own words to create a version of themselves with respect to their tastes.

To enable ease of analysis and the potential to look for trends, the research subjects were asked to comment on their likes and dislikes in a few key areas of consumption; music, film, television, websites and celebrities. This draws upon the areas featured in studies into taste cultures by Bourdieu (2010) and Bennett et al. (2009) and also builds on the findings from the ethnography at City High to ensure that the categories were relevant to the respondents' lives. In addition to this, rather than asking participants to give responses to specific genres, as the Bennett et al. (2009) study did, I asked respondents to write any text that they (dis)liked within a 200-character limit. This follows the idea that online, 'writing is an essential component for performing identity' (Thomas 2004: 367). By opening up the responses so that any words could be written I achieved a far greater breadth of potential responses than other approaches may have been able to. For example, in the Bennett et al. (2009) study participants were only asked to comment on particular genres (at the survey stage) rather than to offer their expressions freely. As Figures 1.3 and 1.4 show respondents were given maximum possible freedom of expression within the context of the identity pages. I also included a blank box, where respondents had the freedom to write any other things that they liked or disliked independent of the categories I offered them – this could include any other area of their lives they wanted to share.

In total I received 78 eligible responses, of which the majority described their gender within the existing gender binary. Thirty-eight respondents described themselves using words that denote a male identity and 38 described their gender using words that denote a female identity – a further two respondents used terms and words that denoted a gender identity outside of the binary. The year of birth of respondents ranged from 1995 to 1998, with the youngest being 13 at the time of data collection and the oldest being 16 years old. The identity pages were closed for further submissions in January 2012 in order for analysis of the data to be undertaken.

These identity pages were then used as a form of elicitation with the focus groups that followed. In these conversations the responses given to the identity pages allowed me to explore the regulatory role that taste plays, as well as to engage with cultures of meaning-making during youth.

Focus Groups

The focus groups were the final of the three methods adopted in this study to explore the (re)production of gender in contemporary youth taste cultures. Silva and Wright (2005) have argued persuasively for the use of focus groups as a method for analysing taste and social position, writing that group discussion allows for the contextualised construction of meaning to be made explicit. Furthermore, focus groups give researchers the opportunity to access a diverse 'collective experience and collective meanings' (Gauntlett 2007: 15) and allow us to witness how 'group members collaborate on some issue[s], how they achieve consensus (or fail to) and how they construct shared meanings' (Stewart, Shamdasani and Rook 2007: 112). Focus groups therefore allow us to capture some of the 'richness and complexity with which people express, explore and use opinions' (Myers and Macnaghten 1999: 174), something crucial to our understanding of the role that taste plays in the (re)production of gender. The final point that I want to make about the usefulness of focus groups in studies such as this (that concern gender, youth and taste) is that when it comes to taste cultures it is in collective spaces that distinction is generated (Silva and Wright 2005: 241).

As I show in the following chapter, young people are fearful of saying that they like the 'wrong' thing for fear of being 'shunned'. The strength of focus groups can therefore be found in their ability to facilitate group interaction, whereby the working out of legitimate or illegitimate opinions can be seen (Silva and Wright 2005: 250). Of course it is important to note that 'there are clearly ways that focus groups are not like a casual conversation between friends' (Myers and Macnaghten 1999: 175), but in working with pre-existing year groups where the participants already knew each other, in this research this disjuncture has been minimised, at least in part. This is because by drawing on pre-existing social groups researchers are able to explore the 'discursive practices surrounding group norms' (Frankland and Bloor 1999: 153). As the groups from this study were pre-existing it allowed me to see how they already negotiate and (re)produce gender discourses.

Conducting the Focus Groups

Focus groups took place with four different groups across three sites with 13 sessions in total, yielding around ten hours of voice and video data. The schools that participated were City High, Outskirts High and Girls High. All of the groups were co-ed except for the all-female group at Girls High and all of the groups were scheduled during the participants' timetables. One of the benefits of school-based focus groups is that the participants already know one another, be friends with other group members or at least know them from the classes or shared school spaces.

An outline of the participants, their schools and the sessions they took part in can be found in the table below:

Researching Youth Taste Cultures

Table 1.1 Participants' schools and sessions attended

Group	School	Number of Sessions	Participants
1	City High	4	Erica, Flora, Jenny, Joe, Leticia, Mel, Pedro, Philly, Portia, Reuben.
2	City High	4	Anwar, Josh, Juan, Lauren, Mary, Naomi, Phoebe, Rachel, Sara.
3	Outskirts High[2]	3	Anna, Chloe, Eliza, Katherine, Tom, Troy.
4	Girls High	2	Bea, Bella, Chocoholic, Clove, Effie, Melark, Owls, Primrose, Rue.

The participants from the groups at City High and Outskirts High were from a low socio-economic background, all working or lower-middle class. The majority of participants from Girls High are from middle class and higher backgrounds, owing in large part to the high fees that this private school charges. The majority of participants are white, in much the same way that the majority of the population of Norfolk are white (the 2011 census recorded that the Black and Minority Ethnic population of Norfolk was 7.6 per cent). Of the five non-white identities, participants' background were varied, including South-Asian, East-Asian, South-East Asian and Middle Eastern. All participants spoke English as their first language.

As you may have noticed, some of the names of the participants listed above are a little unusual. This is because I allowed participants to select their own pseudonyms. Although a number of participants did not mind having their name used, I felt that anonymity was crucial as it offered lifelong security and confidentiality to participants. As Thomson and Holland have reflected (2003), should a participant decide in the future they would like to be anonymised this would require a highly challenging retrospective process of anonymisation for the researcher.

I want to consider for a moment the pseudonyms that the participants chose as they demonstrate the central role that (popular) culture plays in young people's lives. For those that did not select pseudonyms I selected 'regular' and representative names that I felt captured their personalities and backgrounds. At Girls High a large proportion of the group used names that featured in *The Hunger Games*, a popular book that had been adapted into a film released around the same time that the focus groups were taking place.

Other participants chose words (rather than names per se) representing the things that they like, such as 'Owls' and 'Chocoholic', thus further indicating the role that taste cultures play in their everyday lives. At Outskirts High, Troy chose his name because he thought it sounded Roman (at one point he wanted to call himself Maximus) and Anna chose her name because she liked the Disney film *Anastasia* (1997). At City High the majority of participants decided not to come up with their own pseudonyms. Mary had toyed with the name 'Rumpelstiltskin' during the course of all four focus groups before settling on Mary. Mary, along with Juan and Reuben, gave no explanation for her choice of name, while Pedro named himself after the character of the name in *Napoleon Dynamite* (2004), a film that he liked.

Within the group itself a clear structure was implemented in order to make the most of the limited time I had with the participants. This included working through some of the identity pages I had collected during the second stage of data collection (I explain this more fully below). However, I ensured that this structure was flexible and could be adapted to respond to the different groups and their dynamics. This was necessary when I felt the participants found the sessions were becoming predictable. In the latter stages of the groups at City High and Outskirts High I incorporated an additional activity to break up the monotony of the identity page exercise. See the table below for an overview of activities undertaken in each group.

Table 1.2 Focus group activities undertaken with each group, Group One, City High

Session One	Session Two	Session Three	Session Four
Prompt 2; Prompt 8	Prompt 4; Prompt 5	TV Listings Exercise	Prompt 9 Matching-Up Exercise

Table 1.3 Focus group activities undertaken with each group, Group Two, City High

Session One	Session Two	Session Three	Session Four
Prompt 2; Prompt 8	Prompt 4; Prompt 5	TV Listings Exercise	Prompt 9; Matching-Up Exercise

Table 1.4 Focus group activities undertaken with each group, Outskirts High

Session One	Session Two	Session Three
Prompt 2; Prompt 8	Prompt 4; Prompt 9 TV Listings Exercise	Prompt 5 Matching-Up Exercise

Table 1.5 Focus group activities undertaken with each group, Girls High

Session One	Session Two
Prompt 4; Prompt 5	Prompt 2; Prompt 8; Prompt 9 Matching-Up Exercise.

I will now provide an overview of each of the activities that took place in the focus groups: Prompt Exercises, TV Listing Exercise, and Matching-Up Exercise.

Identity Page Prompts

One of the great benefits of collecting the identity pages was that I was able to access authentic youth tastes and present them as a form of elicitation in the focus groups. I selected eight identity page profiles and used them as prompts, taking all of the taste culture information and presenting it on sheets that I handed to participants. I then asked them to discuss the tastes of the person and to guess what gender they thought the person was based on these tastes.

The prompts were constructed to mirror the identity pages but with the avatar and colour removed so that only the participant's tastes were used to guess gender. In all cases I ensured that none of the content was edited, and thus the writing style, language and grammar all remained as they appeared on the identity pages. Some of the focus group participants commented on how they felt that a person that was 'one of them' filled out the sheets. An example of one of the prompts that I used as a form of elicitation in the focus groups can be seen below.

Through this I explored how young people responded to the tastes of their peers. This is because my interest has been in how the tastes that people choose to articulate are read and responded to,

Girls Like This, Boys Like That

and, through this, how ideas of gender appropriate taste are discursively (re)produced.

In order to get an instant response we went around the room where participants said what their 'gut responses' to the question were, and then how their ideas changed or did not change as conversation and collective understandings were worked through. What I found refreshing was that across the focus groups participants were happy to disagree with one another, providing rich data for analysis. As my interest is in discursive (re)production, my focus was on talk and how young people spoke about the tastes of others, and at times themselves. As the only information that the participants had to go on was the likes and dislikes of the prompt-writer, discussions that were directly relevant to the research questions emerged. I looked at how young people constructed their views about taste and gender, as well as how notions of what was appropriate with respect to gender, were articulated. Knowing what gender (in)appropriate texts are, as well as how participants responded to them, helped me to see how

Television I like...

Glee, Britains Got Talent, Friends, Doctor Who, Wife Swap, vampire diaries.

Television I dislike...
Emmerdale

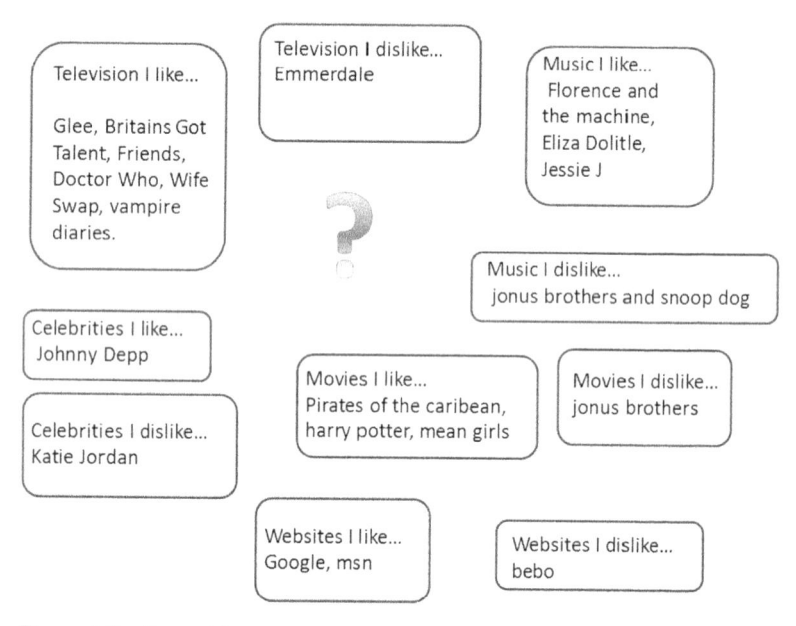

Music I like...
Florence and the machine, Eliza Dolitle, Jessie J

Music I dislike...
jonus brothers and snoop dog

Celebrities I like...
Johnny Depp

Celebrities I dislike...
Katie Jordan

Movies I like...
Pirates of the caribean, harry potter, mean girls

Movies I dislike...
jonus brothers

Websites I like...
Google, msn

Websites I dislike...
bebo

Figure 1.5 Prompt 2

taste (re)produces gender. What was particularly beneficial about the use of prompts was that it allowed participants to think through the nuances of gendered taste and to respond to them. For example, one particular cultural preference may not be necessarily gender (in)appropriate, but when combined with other tastes it may become problematic. For a discussion of this see Chapter 4 where I discuss participants' talk of a combination of boys' tastes being 'just too girly'. Thus the ways in which these judgements were responded to allowed me to see not only *what* cultural texts were deemed gender (in)appropriate, but also *why* they are and in what context.

Television Listings Exercise

The second activity that I carried out with the groups at City High and Outskirts High involved handing out photocopies of pages of *What's On TV* (Time Inc. UK) and asking them to talk about what is considered 'okay' to watch and what isn't. This activity grew from the desire to keep participants engaged in the focus groups and thus offer an alternative to the prompts. I provided a copy of some television listings (*What's On TV*, 2-9 July 2012) and asked them to imagine that they were new at school. In each session the same prompt was handed out, which included six pages of television listings from Monday 2 July 2012 (see Figure 1.6). I asked participants to write down (see Figure 1.7) and be prepared to talk about what television programmes (or films or music) they would comfortably say they watched the night or weekend before, and what ones they would not say they like and why. The aim of this was to have conversations that centred on the collective understandings of what was considered appropriate or not in the context of their school.

This exercise provided a wealth of information about what was considered appropriate or not. It was also in this session where participants were most likely to defend their individual agency and their right to like what they like (as alluded to in Figure 1.7). A strength of using television listings is that they are an everyday part of culture, and thus even if the particular publication is not familiar to the participant, television scheduling often is, and thus participants were readily able to engage in conversation.

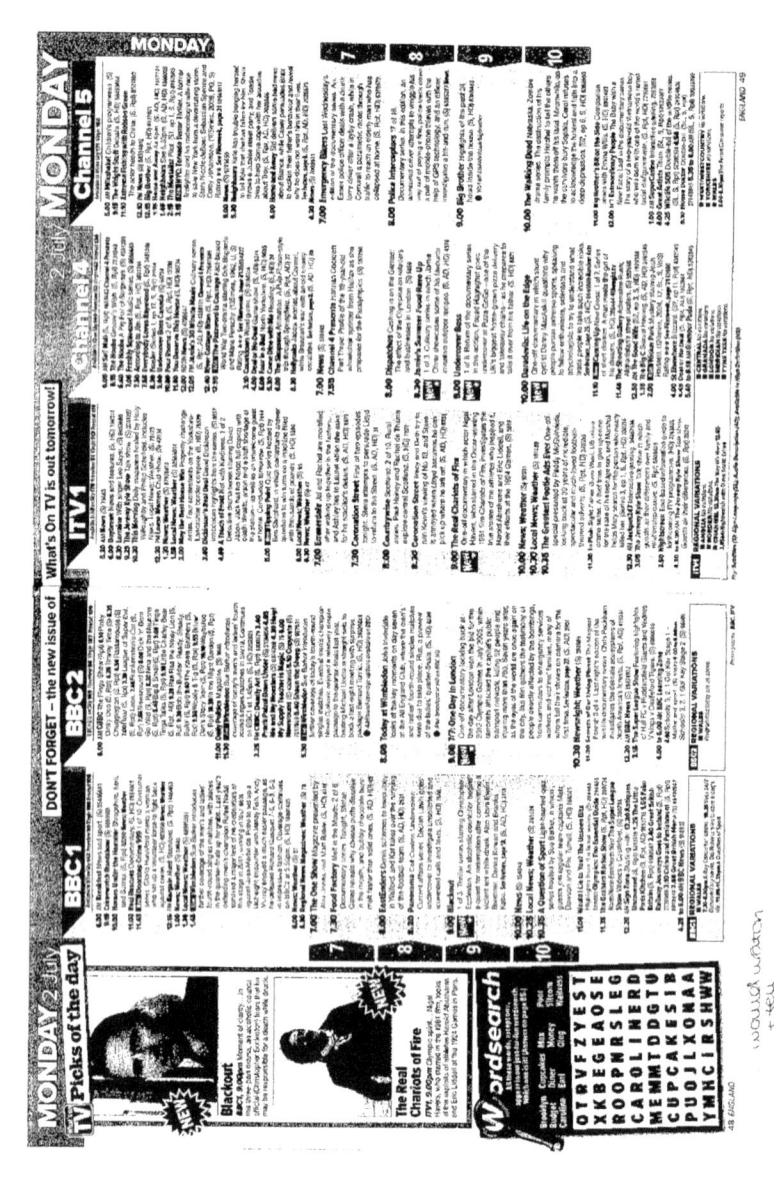

Figure 1.6 TV listings exercise example

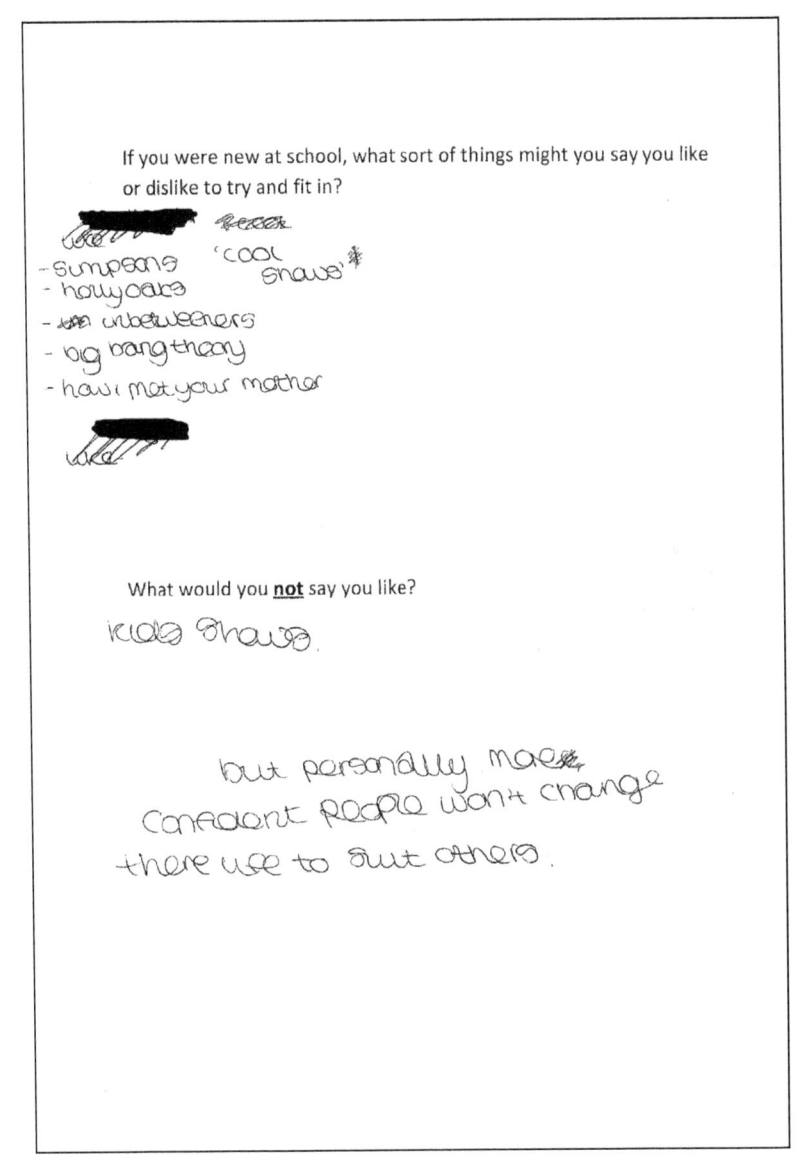

If you were new at school, what sort of things might you say you like or dislike to try and fit in?

▬▬▬▬▬
- simpsons   'cool shows' *
- hollyoaks
- ~~the~~ inbetweeners
- big bang theory
- how i met your mother
▬▬▬▬▬

What would you **not** say you like?

kids shows.

but personally make confedent people won't change there use to suit others.

Figure 1.7 Exercise worksheet example – participant names redacted

Matching-Up Exercise

The final exercise that was used to elicit conversation in all of the groups was the 'Matching-Up Exercise'. This activity was born out of participants' desire to know if their guesses of the prompt-writers' genders were 'correct'. I had initially decided not to reveal the genders of the respondents, as my philosophical position is one that posits that there is no 'right' or 'revealable' gender, but the participants were persistent in their requests and so I decided to build it into a focus group session. Considering that gender studies research has emancipatory potential, one of the outcomes from 'revealing' the respondents' genders would potentially be to challenge (or of course confirm) participants' conceptions of what tastes are or are not appropriate on the grounds of gender.

In all of the groups the matching-up exercise was the final activity undertaken. I incorporated the 'revelation' of the respondents' genders into the focus groups by returning all of the prompts that the participants discussed along with small cut-outs that had the gender that the prompt-writer described themselves as and another with their year of birth. The reason for using both of these was to see what, when given options, discourses of age and gender would be (re)produced. This final activity was especially interesting as some gender norms were troubled, with the discussion of the descriptor 'inbetweener' providing a fascinating insight into how young people make sense of the gender binary.

With each participant having a copy of the prompts, along with the age and gender descriptors, I asked them to work on their own to match the prompt with the descriptors. I asked them to work alone rather than together as I was keen to see what their individual responses would be after a series of conversations. This also allowed me to observe how participants negotiated their opinions alongside the collective understandings, to see if they were (re)produced or troubled in some way. At the end, when I 'revealed' the gender of the prompt-writer, further valuable data was collected, particularly when participants' guesses were challenged by the 'reality'. In these moments the regulation of taste on the grounds of gender could be most clearly observed.

Looking Forward: Designing Research Methodologies for Youth Taste Culture Research

Methodological approaches to youth research must respond to diversities in the experience of youth – especially in terms of cultural consumption, taste and gender. Methods used need to account for both individualistic experiences of taste and collective ones. Too little popular culture research has been undertaken with audiences, perhaps because it asks hard questions about how we can ever really *know* audiences, but this is nevertheless a challenge that we should grapple with. As Helen Wood has written, 'it is time that advances in post-structuralist thought are made to speak to our methodological approaches in feminist media studies' (2009: 111). Taste cultures can be difficult to capture empirically, but this should not be a reason to leave them unexplored. In terms of audience studies more broadly, I am keen to encourage researchers to think creatively and reflexively about how they engage with their participants. The three-method approach that I have taken here can be used to interrogate the cultural lives of people from a range of backgrounds. As I will show in the chapters that follow, rich and nuanced understandings of people's engagement with popular culture can be captured when we think carefully about the methods that we use.

2

Fitting in at School: The Context of Youth Taste Cultures

Within the West, high school is a space that holds continued cultural resonance. At times I find myself reflecting on my experiences at high school, the good and the bad, and I take pleasure in engaging with popular cultural texts that speak to these experiences. Countless Hollywood films have resold us our anxieties about the sense of regulation encountered at high school. From the comedies of *Easy A* (2010), *Superbad* (2007), *Mean Girls* (2004), *Clueless* (1995) and *Fast Times at Ridgemont High* (1982), as well as pretty much anything made by John Hughes or starring Molly Ringwald in the 1980s, to the indies of *Ghost World* (2001) and *Rushmore* (1998), to the dark comedy of *Heathers* (1988), and the drama of *Dead Poet's Society* (1989), to the horror of *Carrie* (1976; 2013) and the updated Shakespeares of *10 Things I Hate About You* (1999) and *Get Over It* (2001) these films seem to have timeless appeal. What makes these types of films so common and so enduring across genres is their ability to capture a collective experience that is familiar to so many of us in the West.[1]

Either as adults looking back, or contemporary youth relating now, one of the reasons for the success of such films is their ability to capture the anxieties, pleasures and difficulties of being at high school. Most importantly they capture (at least in part) the complexities of fitting in, of conforming and of rebelling, and whether we identify vaguely or fully, these films speak to the feelings that accompany this experience that millions of people in the West experience (see for example, Bulman 2005; Driscoll 2011; Shary 2002). It is this enduring anxiety of 'fitting in' to which I now turn, interrogating how young people negotiate this during high school and the ways in which this high school space that I call 'hyper-regulatory' (re)produces subjects.

Appropriateness in Contemporary Youth Taste Culture

In this chapter I discuss *why* young people's tastes matter, and *how* and *why* it is that young people (re)produce discourses of appropriate taste. By asking these questions I reveal young people's motivations behind articulating what I call 'appropriate taste', and I discuss some of the consequences of transgression. To do this I draw on experiences that the participants described as either having specifically happened to them, or their hypotheses of what might happen in particular and/or imagined situations. Both their direct experiences and their expectations can tell us much about the discursive regulation that takes place during youth.

The body of academic literature that has examined taste cultures has indicated that processes of distinction are at play and people distinguish what types of people other individuals are on the basis of taste (see Bennett et al. 2009; Bourdieu 2010; Bryson 1996). Because of this, I posit that people regulate what they say they like or dislike on the basis of wider discourses of what is 'appropriate'. By regulation I mean, as Judith Butler does, 'to become regular' (2004: 40), whereby individuals may either censor or select what they say they like or how they act, based on the understanding of discourses of what is considered appropriate or permissible within a particular context. It is thus through regulatory discourses that gender is (re)produced. In thinking about this in relation to gender it is therefore useful to consider the work of Butler, who states:

> Thus, a restrictive discourse on gender that insists on the binary of man and woman as the exclusive way to understand the gender field performs a regulatory operation of power that naturalizes the hegemonic instance and forecloses the thinkability of its disruption.
>
> (Butler 2004: 43)

Fitting in at School

The audience can be thought of in a dual manner in terms of taste cultures then, as both the audiences of the text and the audiences of the performance of taste articulation. The audience is regulative because it (re)produces discourses that remind individuals (and thus themselves and others) of what is gender appropriate through the problematisation of particular articulations of taste that may be made. In this way taste is regulated, and my interest is in the ways in which this regulation takes place on the grounds of gender through discourses of appropriateness.

In particular I am interested in the expressions of taste that are made and discussed in group settings, because collective understandings are central to discursive (re)production. Kundu has argued that '[s]ome tastes and judgements related to taste may be more acceptable and legitimate than others: they could be called the dominant tastes' (2011: 15), and I am thus interested in the gendering of what may be understood as 'dominant tastes'. As part of this I am also interested in how young people negotiate their expressions in relation to these dominant discourses.

Questions of identity (re)production and taste articulation could be applied to any socio-cultural group with any identity (and I urge these questions to be asked in future research), but my interest in this book is in young people and gender. In thinking about gender appropriate taste, Wilska (2003) makes a pertinent point, arguing that youth is an important period in one's life as it is during youth that one has the opportunity to become an independent consumer, and that as a result of this 'the pressures for keeping up with the "legitimate" styles have never been as strong as they are now' (2003: 443). Rather than thinking about taste specifically, Wilska considers the need to be consuming the right things, and this is ultimately about *taste* because by actively and openly consuming something, you are displaying (even if indirectly) a preference for a particular text or item. Thus, what you consume, that is not only consume by *openly* consume in a way that other people can observe, plays a role in the (re)production of identity. When talking about music, Leung and Kier argue that '[y]oung people often use music to reflect their individual characteristics' (2010: 681). By aligning themselves with particular cultural texts young people can 'say' things about who they are, thereby producing a particular version of their identity. From this perspective then, mundane and everyday activities, such as expressing a preference for a particular cultural text, matter. We need to think beyond cultural consumption and look specifically at taste, as it is through a focus on taste that we can start to understand how these mundane articulations (re)produce identities. Taste is communicative, establishing networks, relationships and status (see Bryson 1997). This is not least because we can think about how identities are regulated and (re)produced through forms of taste because '[t]aste or *judgement* are the heavy artillery of symbolic violence' (Moi 1991: 1026, emphasis in original).

Regulating Taste at High School

The exploratory ethnography coupled with the focus groups (detailed in the previous chapter) provided an understanding of contemporary youth taste. I found that schools were not only a legitimate site of study, but a fruitful one too. This is because articulations of taste and cultural consumption were present across the school day. In addition to this, I found that school was also a space where tastes were regulated through discourses of appropriateness. The discussion of 'Mudhoney or Slipknot' detailed in the previous chapter demonstrates the ways in which taste is regulated and regulative, and thus discursively productive, in the high school context.

Findings

The identity pages revealed the diversity of taste within youth cultures and, while useful in providing a picture of what taste in youth looks like, they tell us very little about how these tastes are translated into the lived realities of young people. I show here how important the working out of these taste cultures is – to both young people and those seeking to understand their cultures. In the following chapters I elucidate how these meanings are played out in the (re)production of gender, while in this chapter I provide an overview of what it is like to be young and at high school and why navigating appropriateness is so important.

One of the central elements to understanding how and why taste matters in terms of the lives of young people is their position in high school. This is because the participants discuss high school in ways that show it to be what I term a 'hyper-regulatory space'. Participants described a concern with not fitting in as being a big part of why they think high school is different to spaces associated with other generations. Being *young* is therefore central to how and why taste plays an important role in young people's experiences of gender (along with other facets of their identity). This is because young people feel that their tastes matter in terms of how they are viewed by other people.

Also in this chapter I complicate ideas of hierarchy at high school, drawing on the participants' experiences of high school as being more loosely organised than that. Participants generally describe school as being organised in a way that leads to most of them wanting to 'fit in' in a general sense. It is therefore less about being 'cool', and more about 'not being marginalised'. Coolness, I argue, plays a role in the experiences that young people have in terms of taste, but coolness is not inherently connected with 'appropriateness' when it comes to gender. A taste articulation could therefore be uncool but nevertheless be understood as gender appropriate.[2] This demonstrates the nuances of youth taste cultures and the methodological significance of speaking to young people directly as a means of elucidating these complexities.

School as Hyper-Regulatory

Due to the high number of young people occupying the space, the repetition of the daily routines and the ways in which it is organised into cohorts (requiring that young people spend long periods of time alongside one another), I argue that high school is a hyper-regulatory space. A significant element of regulation can be understood as either the self-censoring or selection of what one says or how one acts based on one's understanding of discourses of what is appropriate or permissible within a particular context. Regulation is also enacted when individuals are witnessed transgressing the boundaries of what is appropriate. This can either take place overtly or innocuously. To follow Butler then, a large part of regulation is about being 'regular' (Butler 2004: 40), and so with hyper-regulation the importance of 'getting it right' ('being regular' through appropriate articulations) is heightened. Getting it right is about regulation as it requires knowledge of the context, of what is permissible, as well as ensuring that what is articulated is appropriate (and thus *not* articulating something inappropriate for the context). In many ways it mirrors what Sarah Thornton found in her seminal investigation of club cultures, that the articulation of specialised knowledge is a form of subcultural capital, which is 'embodied in the form of "being in the know"' (Thornton 1995: 12). I suggest that a similar form of regulation occurs outside of subcultures, with self-censorship common in high schools and becoming observable when people select what they say they like and dislike.

I make the claim that school is a hyper-regulatory space based on a number of conversations that took place in the focus groups as well as some observations made during the exploratory ethnography. Many of the participants felt that they were constrained in what tastes they could articulate at school, with discourses of what may or may not be appropriate having a regulatory impact.[3] The participants compared this to how they imagined adulthood would be, which was discussed as being less restrictive.[4] On the whole participants imagined that during adulthood the things that they said they liked or disliked would have less of an impact on their day-to-day experiences. There were two logics that framed this thinking; the first was that older people 'mature' to be more accepting (of both their own tastes and those of others). The second logic was that adults aren't 'trapped' in a space like school, and thus adults can 'get away from' the people who render their tastes problematic. While discussed more widely, this idea is encapsulated in a statement made by Pedro at City High:

> Pedro: As you get older, you get your own interests, and you're not afraid to have your own thing, like, when you're younger you just sort of go with the flow a bit more, you just want to fit in and stuff.
>
> (City High, Group One, Session One)

When young people imagine adulthood they therefore see it as a space that is free from regulation in comparison to their own experiences within the context of school. This indicates that, comparatively, they do not see their own taste cultures as being free and accepting. For example, Phoebe commented that 'you get more independence when you're older' (City High, Group Two, Session Three). In addition to gaining independence, in a different group Erica commented that 'you sort of get more confidence as you get older' (City High, Group One, Session One), suggesting that this feeling of confidence is not one that she currently experiences. Comments such as these demonstrate that confidence in their tastes, and the independence to articulate them without fear of being rejected, are not common experiences for these young people. I argue that this is because school plays a central role in their lives and school is a hyper-regulatory space. Adulthood is therefore understood by these participants as offering the potential to retreat from the pressures experienced at school. For example, Pedro said that 'when you're older, like, you can sort of get away from most people that would be judgemental and stuff, but say, you're always in their lessons' (City High, Group One, Session One). Pedro's comments show that young people feel it is not easy to get away from their peers, something that he did not imagine to be a problem faced by adults. This provides further support for the claim that school is a hyper-regulatory space, as regulation – either experienced or imaginary – is ever-present. This demonstrates the need for research to be conducted into youth taste cultures. We should be examining them because young people express feeling restricted in the tastes that they can articulate, which raises questions about the grounds on which such articulations may be problematised. One of the outcomes of these discursive practices is the (re)production of gender, but it is reasonable to imagine that the same processes occur with respect to other identities – and I urge that such research be undertaken.

The need to 'fit in' means that these young people feel their tastes are regulated, being deemed either appropriate or not. This follows Miles, Cliff and Burr (1998), who found that particular consumption choices allowed young people to feel that they fit in with their peers, with consumer goods providing 'resources by which such acceptability can be achieved' (1998: 93). It is my position that one does not even need to *buy* the goods in many cases, and thus simply aligning oneself with a text/item by articulating a preference for it can serve a highly similar purpose. This is particularly important to consider when thinking about young people, as many have highly limited economic resources through which to *buy* goods, leading to an increased significance of the symbolic. However, we can only make sense of the motivation to fit in and to align with gender appropriate texts when we consider the consequences of *not* fitting in. Participants across the focus groups offered a range of examples for why it is bad to display 'inappropriate taste,' and how different forms of regulation occur.

'Shunned': The Consequences of Inappropriate Articulations

For those at City High being bullied was seen to be a direct consequence of inappropriate tastes. Meanwhile, participants at Outskirts High used the word 'shunned' to describe such consequences. Shunned is a useful word to adopt as it is not only a word used by young people themselves (considered to be important for Thorne, 1993), but also because it captures the processes of exclusion that are described by the participants. The term 'shunned' also recognises the social consequences of transgression without the *intent* for harm that is implied through use of the word 'bullying' (Smith, Madsen and Moody 1999: 268). The focus is therefore on what happens if an inappropriate taste is articulated, and knowing this can help us to understand why so many people are motivated to articulate 'appropriate' taste as a consequence.

Group Two at City High, in particular, discussed how shunning and bullying played a central role in the experiences of young people and their reasons for wanting to fit in. They also described how if one was already shunned one would need to be very careful with how and what one demonstrates judgements toward in the future. This is because if an individual was already on shaky ground having displayed a taste articulation rendered inappropriate (e.g. a boy had articulated a preference for something deemed feminine like the film *Twilight* (2008)), then one would likely find the teasing to be exacerbated – at times to the level of outright bullying.

At Outskirts High, Anna used the word 'shunned' to describe someone who had been popular, but had since lost their social position as a result of something they had said. Being shunned is therefore (potentially) different to being bullied, because the term 'shunned' suggests a collective social rejection of someone who had at one point in time 'fit in', whereas someone may experience being bullied having never held higher social status at school, nor may this bullying take place within the context of the collective. Through the discussions it seemed to me that being shunned was a public rejection that could be playfully or seriously enforced, and in the case of the former could be temporary rather than permanent. Whether playful, serious, temporary or permanent, being shunned is a collective discursive process that highlights the importance of appropriateness to all

Fitting in at School

in the community. The consequences of failing to adhere to the discourses of appropriate taste can therefore lead to a collective form of social rejection and symbolic exclusion. When I asked those at Outskirts High to talk about *how* this exclusion is enacted, participants identified a range of techniques:

> Eliza: Shout, scream, laugh, giggle, make up names.
> Anna: Push around, shove.
> Chloe: Get stereotyped.
> Eliza: Yeah and tell their friends, spread that they like a certain thing.
> Katherine: Yeah, spreading it, that's like the biggest thing probably.
> Anna: That is the worst.
> Eliza: Yeah, spreading it.
>
> (Outskirts High, Session Two)

Thus, while instances of physical violence were mentioned as a regulatory force, the overwhelming forms of rejection were symbolic. In this discussion they said that 'spreading it' was the 'biggest' and 'worst' thing that could result from an inappropriate taste articulation. 'Spreading it' involves gossiping across the cohort so that everyone is made aware of the individual's tastes. It is important to note that while these practices are described as some of the outcomes of inappropriate taste, I am cautious not to suggest that they are the *automatic* outcomes, and to emphasise that context is an incredibly important factor. As I show later, there are times when otherwise inappropriate tastes could be read as appropriate, or at the very least 'not problematic'. Nevertheless, the *potential* for these outcomes (for a young person in a space like a high school) is good motivation to articulate appropriate tastes. Keen on understanding gendered dynamics of taste regulation, I asked participants to elaborate on whether spreading it was different for boys and girls. This line of thinking was informed by prior research which has found that boys have often been associated with physical forms of violence (Frosh, Phoenix and Pattman 2002) while verbal forms of abuse have been associated with girls (Guendouzi 2001). I was therefore somewhat surprised to hear that 'spreading it' it was prevalent amongst boys as well as girls:

> Interviewer: Is that for boys or girls?
> Anna: Both.

Eliza:	I'd say more boys than girls.
Katherine:	Yeah I'd say more boys than girls but both.
Eliza:	When it comes to TV programmes boys spread it more than girls.
Katherine:	Yeah, like, oh my god so and so watches this.
Chloe:	And then they link it to things to make it worse like, yeah.
Katherine:	It's like a Chinese whisper it gets worse and worse as it goes down the line like.

(Outskirts High, Session Two)

This conversation also reveals that as part of spreading it, the story can be linked to other things to make it worse (Chloe), which shows that a series of inappropriate tastes may be linked together – having a more damning impact on the individual involved. When I said above that spreading it might not be an automatic outcome of an inappropriate taste articulation, it may be the case that the odd *one* could go unpunished, but a second or especially more would likely not. This conversation also reminds us of the role that the school plays in providing a regulative space where these discourses are (re)produced. As I discuss below, the participants are somewhat reflexive about how arbitrary these discourses of appropriateness are, but they nevertheless acknowledge their importance and are at least complicit in (re)producing them. This reminds us of the importance of contemporary youth research, as it is in the hyper-regulated period of youth that the anxieties of performing appropriate taste are heightened, having considerable impact on how young people (re)present themselves and how they respond to the tastes of others.

What I have argued thus far in this chapter is that young people live within a hyper-regulated space, where not being shunned is motivation for articulating appropriate taste. However, this tells us little about the wider context of youth culture, and this is necessary to consider in capturing the complexities of youth when interrogating their tastes.

Fitting into What?

Fitting in is important to young people, but in this section I want to show that the young people that I spoke to were not necessarily interested in 'being cool' and/or climbing up some kind of social ladder in a way that we might expect. On the whole the participants were suspicious of the

Fitting in at School

'cool kids' and instead discussed just wanting to be 'accepted'. This is important when thinking about taste cultures, as the absence of an aspirational hierarchy distinguishes the context of contemporary youth from Bourdieu's field (2010). Instead, participants discussed simply wanting to 'fit in' with their peers and operate without being shunned.

Although there was a general acceptance in the focus groups that they didn't want to be shunned, participants were nevertheless uneasy about wanting to appear cool. This can be partly connected to Thornton's claim that '[n]othing depletes capital more than someone trying too hard' (1995: 12). While there were a number of disparaging comments made about those who had been shunned and were thus excluded from fitting in, a fair number of disparaging comments were also made about those that were recognised as being 'cool'. The most common criticism was that cool people were 'sheep' who 'followed trends' – words that were notably mentioned in *all* of the focus groups. Interestingly within the all-female group at Girls High there was a comment made about cool people within their context: 'the cool group's sort of like the sporty sort of people' (Session Two). Given that I discuss in Chapter 4 that sport is associated with boy culture, such a comment indicates the universal value of masculine cultures above the feminine. The Girls High group also thought that those at state schools were cooler than them, raising interesting questions about assumptions of working-class 'authenticity' in relation to coolness (see Skeggs 2004b).[5]

In a different group Lauren spoke of her difficulty in talking about what was 'cool' in relation to what she thought was 'good', saying 'yeah, I dunno, coz what is *cool* is what other people think is good, and then what's good is what *I* think is good' (City High, Group Two, Session Two). This complicates our ideas of taste because Lauren draws a distinction between what she understands to be the dominant tastes and her own tastes. However, in my observations Lauren's tastes were rarely troubling in terms of gender. I therefore understand the 'cool' to operate differently to the 'appropriate'. To elaborate, something could be cool and gender appropriate, but something gender appropriate need not be cool. This is because cool is connected to the hierarchy, whereas appropriateness is about fitting in.

The idea that 'cool' operates differently to appropriateness was evident in a number of conversations, and making assumptions about what can or should be considered cool within contemporary youth culture is perilous as 'what's cool changes really quickly' (Anna, Outskirts High, Session One). When we consider this in relation to gender and appropriateness, I argue that we *could* make tentative assumptions as to what could be considered gender appropriate. This is due to the discursive gendering of both audiences and cultural texts (something I explore in much more depth in the chapters that follow). Given the persistence of gender as a category I argue that what's *gendered* does not change that quickly. Therefore when we think of the discursive (re)production of gender in taste articulation it is perhaps not useful to explore popularity and coolness, as these appear to be somewhat distinct from the issue of gender (in)appropriateness. Examples of how gender is (re)produced through taste articulations can be found in the conversations where participants discussed the ways in which they try to protect themselves from being shunned. These conversations reveal how gender is (re)produced as they show how young people use their knowledge of the context to make sure that they articulate appropriately.

Strategies of 'Fitting In'

Participants discussed a range of strategies and responses to the issue of 'fitting in'. As I have argued above, coolness is not necessarily connected to gender appropriateness, and this means that fitting in should not be confused with 'trying to be cool'. Ultimately, aspirations to be cool were not really discussed by participants, who instead discussed how they simply did not want to be ostracised and/or shunned for their tastes. It is through these processes that gender is discursively (re)produced. In this following section I show that the person who makes the cultural judgement matters, as does who is reading and responding to the articulation. These factors are crucial components in understanding contexts of taste articulation as it is context that plays a significant role in how particular articulations are read.

The person expressing the articulation matters. This is because if they were a long-established member of the community, with a precedent for making appropriate articulations of taste, then they would be less likely to be shunned on the grounds of a one-off inappropriate articulation. However, if someone was new at school, and thus had set no precedent of appropriate taste, then it would be much more likely that they would find their tastes problematised and be shunned by their peers. This is exemplified by Eliza, who said that if one was new at school 'you'd never be in to be pushed out' (Outskirts High, Session Two). This also demonstrates that the 'pushing out' – or shunning – on the grounds of taste is a very real consequence in the lives of young people. One of the reasons we can understand taste as being trickier for those new at school is because they are not likely to be familiar with the specific context as well as the audience(s) of their taste articulation(s). While there may be wider discourses of gender appropriateness, how they are played out may vary in context to context. This reveals the importance of context and is something that was discussed by a number of focus group participants.

Focus group discussions revealed that context was by far the most important factor in terms of how young people negotiated fitting in. This is because different contexts involve different audiences, and different audiences have different relationships with the individual. Knowing the context that you are in is therefore crucial to what is articulated, with Pedro, for example, stating, 'yeah, depends who you're with, you might say different things to different people' (City High, Group One, Session Three). This demonstrates the ways in which individuals regulate themselves, being careful about what they choose to articulate in any given moment. In a different session at City High, Joe discusses context in terms of friendship groups:

> Joe: I think it depends what friendship group you're with [.]
> [Erica nods head]
> Joe: Like if I'm with my close friends, I'll be honest about the music and the films that I like, but if I'm with people that I just hang around with from time to time, and I'm not that confident with them, if I say anything, I might be a bit judgemented if we're still in that phase.
> (City High, Group One, Session One)

As Joe's comments illustrate, not knowing how someone might respond to a particular taste articulation is grounds for cautiously regulating what he might say. It is especially interesting to note that Joe says that he would be 'honest' with his close friends, but not with those he is less confident around. This demonstrates the ways in which he carefully censors and edits his taste articulations depending on the context he is in, and thus the potential for him being 'less honest' in some situations. This logic is continued in discussions held in other groups, with Lauren and Rachel at City High saying:

> Rachel: It depends who you're with like some people I say I do and some people I say I don't, depends on the mood really.
> Lauren: I don't, if I think the people aren't going to agree with me, I just won't say anything.
> (City High, Group Two, Session Three)

It seems that, for the participants, the consequences of making particular articulations of taste outside the safety of their friendships groups (or indeed even within them) may be too costly. Friendship provided a 'safe space' context for participants of all genders, with notably both boys and girls finding the space provided within close friendships to be supportive. This is notable as it demonstrates that boys have a similar experience of support within friendship circles to that of their female counterparts, something that has thus far been theorised as something enjoyed primarily by girls (Hey 1997; Morris-Roberts 2004; Scott 2003). This feeling of support for boys as well as girls is exemplified in the below excerpt:

> Interviewer: So when do you get to have an opinion?
> Leticia: When you get to know them better.
> Pedro: When you get friends.
> Joe: When you feel comfortable with them and you trust them, when, like you can kind of feel like no matter what you say, they'll be alright with it.
> (City High, Group One, Session Two)

Despite this, girls' friendships were nevertheless considered to be much closer than those of boys, a result perhaps of 'feminine' behaviours such as 'caring' and 'emotional maturity' being seen as gender appropriate for girls and thus discursively dominant. This is the topic of discussion at Outskirts High:

> Interviewer: Is it easier for girls or boys to like erm, like things, or admit to liking things?
> Anna: I think it's easier for girls to like things.
> Katherine: Yeah coz girls actually have, like, girls have closer friends –

Fitting in at School

Tom:	– I was shunned –
Katherine:	– because boys don't really have like, friends as such.
Chloe:	Well they have friends but not like the same relationship as.
Eliza:	It's not the same thing.
Katherine:	It's not very close, like, it's just a big group.
Eliza:	It's someone you sit with at lunch and take the mick out of.
Katherine:	Yeah.
Chloe:	I think girls tell more personal things to their friends than –
Katherine:	– yeah girls have like proper friends, I would say girls have more like, well, we're bitchier but we have more kind of friends.
Eliza:	But are we bitchy because we're closer?
Katherine and Chloe:	Yes.

(Outskirts High, Session Two)

The above conversation offers insight into how girls perceive their friendship circles and how they operate in relation to taste cultures. Katherine, agreeing with Anna's comment that it's easier for girls to admit liking things because of the closeness girls share offers a potential reason as to why it's easier for girls to admit liking things. This closeness provides a context of acceptability for girls, which they suggest, and Tom as a witness attests, is not the case for their male counterparts. In discussing this distinction Katherine clarifies that it's not that boys don't have friends (we know that they do as previous conversations have shown), but rather that they understand there to be a qualitative difference in the *sort* of friendship that boys and girls have with members of their own gender.[6] Here, there is an understanding that girls are able to 'tell personal things' to each other and are 'closer', creating a communicative openness that the girls understand as central to the acceptance of their tastes.

While these conversations demonstrate that friendship provides a space for acceptance this is in relation to the wider context of high school, which is much less supportive in comparison. And although it is useful to know this, we still do not know how young people learn what is appropriate – something central to our understanding of the discursive (re)production of identity. While some of the articulations that young people consider inappropriate are drawn from dominant discourses of gender, the appropriateness of others may not be as clear cut. In situations of the latter, young people find themselves in a position where they need to think and respond quickly. Given the complicated terrain of the things young people like in general, it is perhaps not surprising that some participants discussed needing to think on their feet and respond to uncertainty quickly. This draws us back to the work of Erving Goffman, who argues that actors need to draw upon the 'accredited values of society' in order for the performance of identity to be accepted (1971: 45).

In conversations that reflected the challenge posed by uncertainty, participants discussed the importance of knowing what had happened previously in similar contexts as a means of negotiating their taste articulations effectively. Reflecting on precedents therefore helped them to minimise their chances of being shunned on the grounds of inappropriate taste articulations. One way participants discussed doing this would be to let someone else make the articulation first, and to then see what happened:

> Mary: I was gonna say that, erm, I was gonna say that once one person's sorta opened up, oh I'd I really wanna go see that, I think everyone else sort of thinks that, not that copying, but they sort of have that in the back of their mind as well but they don't want to open up.
> [...]
> Rachel: Like on Mary's point as well, people might not feel as though they can say it because they're not sure like who else is going to feel the same way, but like if everyone is going to disagree with them or like tease them about it, but if one person does it, then it might make them feel a bit more like reassured to then do it and know that they're not going to get bullied for it.
>
> (City High, Group Two, Session Three)

Other strategies included asking those you are with what they like, and then responding accordingly:

> Flora: If I was new at school I wouldn't say that I'd watched anything.
> Interviewer: You wouldn't say anything?
> Reuben: Just wait until they say that they like something [.]

Fitting in at School

Erica: Yeah –
Reuben: – and then say ooh yeah I watch that! And then you'd automatically get to [waves hand to gesture 'in'].
(City High, Group One, Session Three)

This approach allows the individual to ensure that they will not be shunned because of their tastes, as they would be following the precedent set by another (accepted) group member (this can be a relatively safe measure providing that the person they are setting a precedence against has been accepted by the group). Another approach discussed was to use a prompt to start a discussion about a particular text as a means of gauging a response. For example, Sara suggested that 'conversations would probably start by seeing an advert somewhere on a bus or a TV' (City High, Group Two, Session Three). Through doing this, the individual has a means of neutrally introducing the text into conversation and finding its value before making a public expression of judgement about it. These strategies highlight the reflexivity of taste articulation, where young people can be seen to be strategically regulating their taste articulations on the basis of what is understood and collectively agreed upon as appropriate.

Not Fitting In

In other groups that I interviewed (especially in the case of Group Two at City High) participants were keen to stress their own independence and agency in their taste articulations. Those that blindly follow the rules – perhaps using the aforementioned self-regulatory practices – were described as 'sheep'. A few participants in Group Two spoke of how they were not interested in 'fitting in' and thus discussed their tastes in ways that could be seen to transgress dominant discourses. For example, Naomi (who had a range of different tastes to her friends – she was really into football and also liked the boy band One Direction) continuously asserted that she would not lie to fit in:

Phoebe: Yeah I'd say what I liked, like what I actually like.
Naomi: I wouldn't lie just to fit in.
(City High, Group Two, Session Three)

Such an approach is also demonstrated in the response written on one of the worksheets (repeated from Chapter 1):

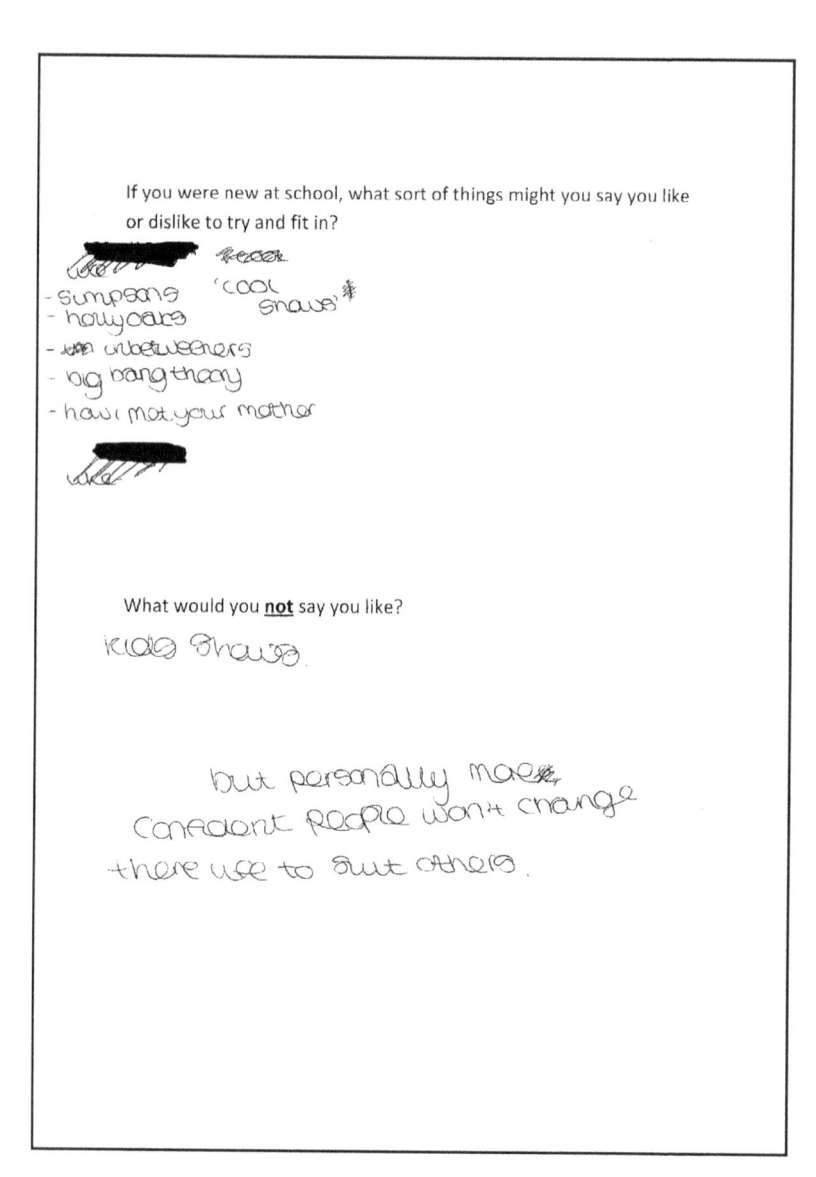

If you were new at school, what sort of things might you say you like or dislike to try and fit in?

- Simpsons 'cool shows'
- hollyoaks
- inbetweeners
- big bang theory
- how i met your mother

What would you **not** say you like?

kids shows.

but personally more confident people won't change there life to suit others.

Figure 2.1 Exercise worksheet example – participant names redacted

Importantly though, Phoebe and Naomi were not shunned within the group. This is because they had precedents set that allowed them to make these transgressions while ultimately not troubling the wider discourses. This is also largely because, as I discuss in Chapter 5, girls have much more freedom in the tastes that they can articulate than boys do; a result of the lower status of femininity and girls' culture (see also Cann 2014). Additionally, although some participants indicated that they may have transgressed appropriateness when emphasising their own agency, it was rare that I saw the troubling of dominant discourses anywhere. This nevertheless exemplifies the extent of regulation in different youth taste cultures, as having to assert that you do not follow the dominant discourses nevertheless demonstrates the existence and prevalence of such discourses in the first place.

Concluding Remarks

In this chapter I have aimed to demonstrate that youth taste cultures are regulatory and to elucidate why young people have a motivation to articulate appropriate taste(s). I have argued that high school is experienced as a hyper-regulatory space by young people. The hyper-regulation of high school means that young people feel pressure to fit in, a result of spending long periods of time feeling they are inside each other's pockets. The result of this is that young people feel restricted in what they can say they like for fear of the social repercussions that would negatively impact their day-to-day experiences. One of these repercussions was to be 'shunned'; a term used by participants at Outskirts High which usefully captures the social exclusion that takes place during youth. Being shunned may be an outcome of inappropriate taste, and knowledge that shunning can happen is itself regulatory. None of the participants wanted to be shunned, and this is understandable as they occupied the same spaces daily, and thus exclusion would be unlikely to be a positive experience for them. The desire not to be shunned in a hyper-regulatory space therefore helps us to understand the motivation for articulating appropriate taste in contemporary youth cultures.

When it comes to what appropriate taste is, and how it can be learned, I have distinguished what is 'appropriate' from what is 'cool'. I have done so as what is 'cool' changes very quickly and while this may be connected to gender in some ways, gender appropriateness is different and almost 'cool-neutral'. This is because gender is discursively inscribed into texts and tastes outside of what may or may not be cool. I have argued that something may be uncool but nevertheless gender appropriate – the nuances of which are the subject of exploration in Chapters 4, 5, and 6.

Context is key to understanding what articulations can be appropriately made. This is because there are some moments where articulation is 'safer' than others, as well as moments where the outcome of a particular articulation is unknown. Drawing on the experiences of the young people from the focus groups, I have shown that if someone has set a precedent for having appropriate tastes then the odd taste that is inappropriate is unlikely to lead to them being shunned. However, if someone is new to the school, then inappropriate tastes may have a bigger impact on their position (or potential position) within the group. Participants discussed that if they were new, or in uncertain situations, then they would need to 'test the water' before expressing an articulation of taste. Regulation on the grounds of taste is therefore widely experienced, demonstrating the importance of exploring the ways in which taste cultures (re)produce identities during youth.

In this chapter I have argued *why* young people's taste cultures matter, and *how* and *why* it is that young people (re)produce dominant discourse. The focus of the remainder of the book is on gender as the (re)produced identity; a focus taken because of the continued and persistent inequalities experienced at the level of gender.

3

What is Gender? Theorising Gender and Young People's Lived Experiences

The certainty of gender has never been as unfixed as it is now. From the game-changing academic work on gender as a performance, from thinkers such as Judith Butler and Jack Halberstam, through shifts in media representations ranging from singers such as Janelle Monáe and Lady Gaga to media texts like *Orange is the New Black* (Netflix 2013 – present) and *TransAmerica* (2005), gender is starting to be understood as much more fluid than what has otherwise been permissible with respect to the rigidity of the male/female binary. In this chapter I outline the ways in which gender has been conceptualised within the academic field, drawing in particular on theories of gender as a performative act. I then go on to explore how this understanding works out in the lived realities of the young people who took part in this study, showing that while young people are open to non-binary conceptions of gender, the persistence of patriarchy makes actually *living* this openness very difficult, leading the gender binary to be (re)produced relatively intact.

Conceptualising Identity

Post-structural identity scholars are indebted to the work of Michel Foucault and his vast oeuvre on power, subjectivity and discourse.

Following the anti-essentialist position, I do not believe that there is an inherent 'essence' to oneself, and thus I do not conceive of identity as fixed within a knowable 'truth'. I align myself with the field of scholars who understand the individual as what Barry calls a 'tissue of textualities' (2009: 63), a fragmented product of discursive cultural construction. Identities are therefore fluid, shifting, changeable and ultimately contextually contingent.

I reject the idea that meanings are fixed, and I am therefore interested in understanding how, despite this lack of fixedness, particular meanings come to be worked out and (re)produced. This follows the idea that identity is a 'complex mix of chosen allegiances' (as discussed by Barry 2009: 140), raising questions about what allegiances are made, at what time, and why. Identity then can be understood as a process of articulation; this is because it is in articulation that these textualities can be known. Crucial to this is Judith Butler's idea that 'identity is a signifying practice' (1990: 145). Taste articulation can be understood as one such signifying practice, as it requires one to not only align and identify with particular subjectivities, but also to dis-identify with others. This follows the important research of Anoop Nayak and Mary-Jane Kehily, who argue that in the context of youth, discursive production forms 'an *organising principle* in peer group relations in school' (2006: 460, emphasis in original). Thinking about discourse as providing an 'organising principle' can therefore help us to make sense of how discourses of gender are (re)produced and can be (temporarily) stabilised in contemporary youth taste cultures.

Discourses are central to social life, providing the means through which to understand not only how identity is (re)produced, but also how particular versions of identity become privileged. Following Stuart Hall's claim that identities are produced *within* rather than *outside* of discourse (2000: 17), there is much that can be gained from an interrogation and deconstruction of the discourses which produce identity. This is because such endeavours reveal what Christine Griffin calls 'sets of rules and practices through which power is legitimated' (1993: 7). Meanwhile, Hall argues that while poststructural accounts tell us much about how subject positions are constructed through discourse, they 'reveal little about why it is that certain individuals occupy some subject positions rather than others' (2000: 23). This is also something discussed by Helen Wood, who has argued that poststructuralist accounts of gender as performance (such as those posited by Judith Butler) are accounts that have 'rarely been brought to bear upon the temporalities of media reception and its links with identity formation' (2009: 6), something that the empirical nature of this book seeks to redress.

(Re)producing Gender

While ideas of masculinity and femininity are often (problematically) rooted within biologically determined accounts of sex/gender (see Cordelia Fine's *Delusions of Gender* (2010) for an excellent deconstruction of the 'science' behind sex and gender), masculinity and femininity are understood as the 'cultural' versions of these biological 'realities'. In her influential early work on the topic, Ann Oakley argued that 'technology has altered the necessity of biology on society, but our conceptions of masculinity and femininity have shown no corresponding tendency to change' (1972: 16). This claim demonstrates the power of discourse in the (re)production of gender, raising questions about how these discourses are sustained, particularly as some 45 years have passed since Oakley first made this claim. It is in asking these questions that we are drawn to Simone de Beauvoir's now iconic assertion that 'one is not born, but rather becomes, a woman' (1972: 301). And although masculinity may exist as culturally superior to femininity under patriarchy, it follows that masculinity is subject to the same discursive (re)production as femininity (Connell 1995; Robb 2007).

However, such accounts continue to operate within binaries, suggesting that female/male and feminine/masculine are the only possibilities for individuals in the (re)production of gender; normalising and assuming a cisgender account in the process. To clarify, the term cisgender is applicable to those whose experience of gender aligns with that which they were assigned at birth. Cis, which means 'on the same side of', is thus conceptually useful for thinking about gender expressions that 'match' the biology/sex of an individual. Cis is a privilege within a society that understands gender as operating within a fixed binary because cisgender people are able to 'be' male or female simply because they have been 'born' and raised as that particular sex (see Serano 2007 for a much fuller and more nuanced account of this privilege). Schilt and Westbrook have argued that gender trouble is therefore rupturing for cisgender people, and so 'normatively gendered tactics that reify gender and sexual difference' (2009: 442) are deployed. It is my contention in this book that tastes are one of these 'gendered tactics' and I am therefore keen to broaden our understanding of gender to draw on queer theory and to think of gender as artificial. With this in mind I ask the question, if one *becomes* a particular gender, what is to say that the gender they become matches their physiology, and indeed what is to say that their physiology is fixed in any kind of knowable 'truth' anyway? To explore these questions in greater depth I now turn to queer conceptions of gender, with the aim of demonstrating why discourse is so important to understanding the (re)production of narrow and binary ideas of gender.

Queering Gender

Queer theorists have been challenging gender for some time now (e.g. Butler 1993; Driver 2008; Halberstam 2005). If gender is an artifice, understanding how this artifice is (re)produced through something as everyday as taste can tell us much about the state of gender in contemporary youth taste cultures. My position is one that understands that gender is an artifice that is (re)produced through iteration, and that taste is used in iteration. Taste is therefore both an articulation and a resource in the performance of gender.

Queer is a useful concept in accounting for the complexities of gender identity as it 'signif[ies] performative dynamics of doing rather than determinate identities' (Driver 2008: 10). This deconstructs the idea of identity being determinate, emphasising instead its constructed nature. For Butler, 'there is no gender identity behind the expressions of gender [...] identity is performatively constituted by the very 'expressions' that are said to be its results' (1990: 25). Iteration helps us to understand how gender is (re)produced within culture despite being an artificial and culturally constructed category. Within queer theory then, emphasis is placed on 'performativity', or 'the ways in which identity is enacted through iterative practices' (Redman 2000: 13). Such thinking troubles determinist accounts of gender.

However, just because I take a poststructural approach to identity, this does not mean that I see the body as meaningless. Rather, the meaning of the body is also not fixed and, as with other aspects of identity, such as gender, the body is an 'idea', an 'inscribed surface of events' (Foucault 1984: 83). If, as I have argued above, identity is a 'series of textualities', then the body is one of the many texts that contributes to identity formation – but it is nevertheless an important one, as it is 'a medium through which the discursive signs of gender are given corporeal significance' (Nayak and Kehily 2006: 468). This is because gender is often attributed on the basis of the body. Following the notable work of Kessler and McKenna (1978), gender is attributed to people on the basic (discursively dominant) understanding that everyone is male or female, and thus gender is commonly attributed to people in a binary form.

Gender as Performance: Performing Gender

While I do not specifically examine the *performance* of gender in this book, but focus instead on the discourses that are employed in *reading* performances, thinking of the performative nature of identity is central to the backbone of this work. In particular Erving Goffman's (1971) dramaturgical account of the presentation of self and West and Zimmerman's (1987) idea of 'doing gender' have provided timeless conceptual tools in the development of gender theory. What makes these works of interest, in addition to the philosophy of Judith Butler, is that they explicate the importance of considering appropriateness and the wider cultural implications of particular identity performances. For example, West and Zimmerman argue that gender is 'the activity of managing situated conduct in light of normative conceptions of attitudes and activities appropriate for one's sex activity' (1987: 127). Goffman's role theory can help us to better understand how this plays out in lived reality, because '[r]oles are defined by expectations and norms, sex roles by expectations attaching to [assumed] biological status' (Connell 2005: 25).

Goffman's dramaturgical accounts of identity as performance can help us to think about the strategies that social *actors* employ to perform 'appropriate' articulations of taste. Furthermore, dramaturgical accounts of identity also highlight the importance of audiences in receiving these performances. For example, Bethan Evans notes that Goffman's work adds to that of Butler because performances of gendered identities are understood not as 'isolated individual performances [...] but are performed for, and received and regulated by others' (2006: 551). What Goffman's theories therefore offer us is a sense of a wider context, a context in which those who receive these performances are also accounted for. This book deals with the audience (in its multiple forms), and it is thus the audience and their collective strategies of sense-making that I am interested in interrogating in relation to contemporary youth taste cultures. In terms of queer theory then, articulations of taste are iterative, and it is only via slippages that gender is troubled. Goffman's work helps us to see the role that the audience plays in identifying these slippages. As I show in the final empirical chapter of this book (Chapter 6), the troubling of gender is 'rupturing' for cisgender people, and thus cisgender people reify gender and sexual differences (see Schilt and Westbrook 2009), helping us to understand the reasons behind gender regulation (such as the regulation of gender appropriate tastes). The symbolic resources that are used in taste exchanges are thus of central importance, as it is through them that we can explore some of the everyday sites of the (re)production of gender.

Queer conceptualisations have been crucial in advancing academic thought on gender, but are somewhat limited in their empirical applicability. 'Doing' gender, to borrow West and Zimmerman's term, involves particular 'appropriate' performances. What can be known as 'appropriate' is discursively (re)produced, and is heavily regulated in the hyper-regulatory space of the high school (see previous chapter for an examination of this process). My aim for the rest of the chapter is to explore how these ideas work in relation to young people's lived experiences of gender. Given that queer theory is more of a radical position existing primarily within the domain of academia rather than in everyday 'real life', it would be reasonable (although not necessarily fair) to imagine that young people do not conceive of gender in such fluid terms. What I will show here is that many young people are open to queer accounts of gender and discuss gender in more fluid terms than I experienced in my own childhood. However, I ultimately show that their geographical location along with the persistence of patriarchy makes actually living these principles much harder. While focus group discussions demonstrated awareness of the possibility of genders that trouble the binary, the potential consequences of transgression were also understood. I show that troubling was usually (re)interpreted through dominant discourses, where 'regular' accounts of the gender binary were (re)produced.

What is Gender?

'I Needed a Gay': Young People's Conceptualisations of Gender

During the course of this research I have found that although participants often made a distinction between sex and gender, they frequently reiterated the 'discoverability' of gender in terms of biology. This is significant because if young people believe that there *is* a discoverable gender, then there would likely be such a thing as gender appropriate taste. Ensuring that your tastes are coherent with the gender that you present as[1] is important in ensuring that you are not shunned in the hyper-regulatory context of high school (see previous chapter).

Given that queer theory, as outlined above, is a more radical position which exists predominately in the domain of academia rather than in 'lived reality' for the majority of people, it is not surprising that focus group participants did not discuss gender in the same way that I do as a gender researcher. I instead found that while many participants were keen to appear progressive in their discussion of gender, accounts limited by binary thinking were nevertheless overwhelmingly (re)produced. Existing work has started to reveal the complexities of gender in youth (for example, see Driver 2008) and it is my contention that by examining how young people understand gender the complexity of gender in youth can begin to be illuminated. Gender is a complex category at the best of times, and I found that young people often struggled to communicate their ideas about it.

As mentioned in the discussion of the methodologies employed in this research (Chapter 1), two of the respondents completing identity pages described their gender identity outside of the male/female binary. These responses came from Respondent 130 who described their gender as 'inbetweener' and Respondent 146 who described their gender as 'i'm confused i have both'. These responses show that gender is experienced outside of the binary for at least some people in the context of the study. This reinforces the need to examine how the gender binary is (re)produced as it is likely to have a significant impact on those who experience gender outside of it. In the focus group discussions I ensured that a variety of genders were considered by including the inbetweener prompt in the sessions. 'Inbetweener' was a gender descriptor written by someone who had attended Boundary High, which was not the site of any of the focus groups. I had purposely included this prompt as it ensured discussion about gender beyond the binary, and it is crucial to note that prior to the matching-up exercise in the final sessions, *none* of the participants from the focus groups used the term 'inbetweener'. Furthermore, *none* of the participants imagined any of the prompt-writers in terms beyond the gender binary – although 'gender confused' was mentioned in one of the sessions. This demonstrates that participants did not readily think of gender outside of the binary until they were prompted to do so, further indicating the prevalence of the gender binary within contemporary youth culture.

Before I discuss how the participants understood gender, I turn to a conversation revealing how being in Norfolk was seen as integral to the participants' development of beliefs and ideas – reminding us of the importance of contextually locating young people within particular geographies.

Gender in Norfolk: Geographically Situating Gender

For participants from Outskirts High being in Norfolk was discussed as playing an important role in how they experienced gender. As described in Chapter 1, 'Research Youth Taste Cultures: The Study', Norfolk is a county marked by its rurality, few major roads service the area and transport connections to other major cities and counties are relatively poor. This was considered to be important by the young people I spoke to. In their conversations I found that participants imagined their peers in bigger cities such as London to be more progressive in their approach to gender, especially in terms of accepting more fluid and queer gender identities. This is exemplified by Eliza who said that, 'they're more accepting [in London]. I don't think it would be as bad as what it is here, because we're so like, secluded' (Outskirts High, Session One). This statement indicates that the gender binary may play a more regulatory role in the lives of young people in Norfolk, with young people's approaches to gender being more, according to Eliza, 'bad'. This is interesting as it was at Outskirts High that I experienced what I considered to be considerable knowledge of alternative gender identities, as the result of a recent Personal Development

Assembly on trans+ identities that they had attended, suggesting that they were perhaps not being fair to themselves.

The Sex/Gender Distinction

The inbetweener prompt was useful in eliciting conversations about the potential for gender outside of the binary, and it was refreshing to find that many of the participants did not employ biologically deterministic accounts of gender in their discussions. For example, Erica made a distinction between sex and gender, saying 'well biologically they are like a boy or a girl but gender is kind of fluid I think, like depending on how you see yourself, I dunno' (City High, Group One, Session Four). While Erica is certainly not confident or certain about what she's talking about, the distinction that she makes between sex and gender is clear. This indicates that young people like Erica certainly have the potential to understand gender as an arbitrary category. However, although these sorts of distinctions were made, we also see in this statement an emphasis being placed on the binary core of gender. This makes the claim that the 'ontological security ascribed to sex and gender allows them to operate as seemingly stable points of reference in an increasingly insecure world' (Nayak and Kehily 2008: 198) a persuasive one in light of the findings that I present here. Furthermore, at Outskirts High, Troy can be seen negotiating the complex cultural/biological framing of gender, saying: 'it depends, gender is just male and female like X and Y chromosomes, but if you want to get into then you've got like the weird stuff like transsexual, asexual, pansexual, that depends who you're going into' (Session Three). This shows that although Troy is open to and acknowledges alternative genders (although some conflation with sexuality is made); the extent to which gender is troubled is limited somewhat by his comment about 'the weird stuff', which discursively renders non-normative binary genders as 'Other'.

An alternative position was offered by Sara from Group Two at City High. Sara was not troubling her own performances of gender, but she did often offer critiques of cisnormativity, and raised questions about why it should *have* to be that girls like one thing and boys another. However, even in the more progressive case of Sara, she nevertheless fell back on biology as a means of 'knowing' gender. For example, in Session Two she

Girls Like This, Boys Like That

challenged Naomi's assumption that Gwyneth Paltrow is an actress (read: female) and not an actor (read: male) in the following exchange:

Interviewer:	Gwyneth Paltrow!
Phoebe:	Who's that?
Interviewer:	Who is that?
Juan:	Don't know.
Sara:	I don't know.
Juan:	Who is that?
Lauren:	Erm, she's blonde, I think.
Rachel:	Never heard of her.
Phoebe:	I might know her by face but not.
Sara:	Yeah I'm useless with names.
Mary:	I'm more good with like the actors, is she an actor? Before I say that yeah.
Naomi:	Actress.
Mary:	Actress.
Naomi:	Female.
Sara:	How do you know?...
Lauren:	I'm trying to think of what she's in.
Sara:	.... She might just be feminine, coz you've seen[2] her?
Naomi:	Not seen her like that! God!
Sara:	How do you know she's a girl then?
Phoebe:	Just, Sara, give it up!
[laughter]	

(City High, Group Two, Session Two)

Meanwhile in Session Four Sara offered a similarly biologically deterministic account of gender when Lauren expressed that she wasn't sure how she'd describe her gender:

Lauren:	I don't know how I'd describe myself, I'm just thinking I don't know how I'd describe myself like, female.
Sara:	I'm going to put this as polite as I can; you have a vagina don't you?
	[group laughter]
Sara:	Then you're a woman!

(City High Group Two, Session Four)

What is Gender?

Such comments were common across the focus groups, highlighting a desire for the certainty and knowability of gender, further supporting Nayak and Kehily's claim for the stability of gender in an unstable world. For example, at Outskirts High Troy discusses trans-female identities saying 'for all intents and purposes, they *think* that they're a woman but they don't have ladyparts'. In the lengthy excerpt that follows the openness that young people have to potentially 'trouble' gender is refreshing, but is nevertheless anchored in some form of biological certainty.

Interviewer:	Well the options I got were female, feminine, girl, boy, male. One person said that they had both and one person said that they were an inbetweener, erm, but here the options that we've got are, two people described themselves as female, one as male, one as a manly male and one as an inbetweener.
Katherine:	What does that mean?
Interviewer:	What do you think it means?
Troy:	A little bit of column A and a little bit of column B.
Eliza:	A trans-gen-der isn't it?
Anna:	Oh the cake in half kinda! Right.
Tom:	Yeah!
Anna:	I have a good description of that.
Troy:	No, it's not.
Katherine:	Are they actually transgender or have they just put that?
Chloe:	They probably just feel that they're both.
Tom:	They're greedy they get both the cakes.
Troy:	Maybe like a tomboy, or him [Tom].
Interviewer:	Because I haven't met this person I don't know exactly what it is that they meant so your understanding of what you think they mean by use of the term inbetweener is as valid as mine.
Anna:	Struggling with their sexuality.
Eliza:	Yeah, I say, yeah.
Troy:	Depends.
Tom:	Metaphorically or literally.
Chloe:	Like Unique on Glee.
Anna:	So, bisexual.
Eliza:	No, coz that's just sexual orientation.

Girls Like This, Boys Like That

Troy:	That's not gender.
Eliza:	No maybe they feel that they don't know if they're a girl that wants to be a boy or boy or should be[.] a[.] girl.
Anna:	Think back to fit what is it called, trans?
Eliza:	There's transgender.
Eliza and Anna:	Transsexual.
Tom:	Anna did you watch it?
Anna:	Yeah, in P.D.
Eliza:	What is a transsexual, I don't even know what those words mean.
Anna:	Transsexual is like …
Katherine:	They like, both sex?
Troy:	No, transsexual wears the clothes of the other sex, but they like the …
Eliza:	… the one they're in …
Troy:	Yeah.
Eliza:	So what are cross-dressers then?
Troy:	It's kind of the same thing. For all intents and purposes, they think that they're a woman but they don't have ladyparts.
Tom:	I don't have ladyparts.
Chloe:	It's like Unique on Glee.
Tom:	What?
Chloe:	Unique on Glee.

(Outskirts High, Session Three)

This conversation also highlights the important role that sex and sexuality education plays alongside popular culture in young people's understandings of gender. The exchange that took place at City High further demonstrates the role that popular culture plays in young people's sex and sexuality education:

Erica:	There was a person on Big Brother who had a sex change at the moment.
Leticia:	No one cares about Big Brother.
Erica:	Yeah well.

(City High, Group One, Session Four)

What is Gender?

To return to the conversation at Outskirts High, while a little clunky in their language, the participants were able to distinguish between gender and sexuality (something that I discuss below as being a common issue in other sites of study) as well an awareness of non-cisnormative gender identities. Importantly though, transfolk are still Othered through use of the distancing/'not us' term, 'they', and, as with Sara, Troy anchors gender in the genitalia of the person in question – 'ladyparts' are seen as a crucial component in 'actually' being a woman. This suggests then that young people understand that there *is* a fixed gender against which they can measure the appropriateness of taste(s). This is because the young people that I spoke to understood gender as ultimately defined by biology (which works in a binary form) and thus this is how their gender attributions are made. Furthermore, Troy disparaged the inclusion of inbetweener as a gender identity saying 'I still can't believe someone actually thought that would be a good idea' (Outskirts High, Session Three). In making this comment Troy reminded all who heard it of the acceptable parameters of gender.

Lived experiences of gender beyond the cisnormative binary were discussed in Group One at City High, demonstrating the nuances and complexities of transgressive gender in a space such as school. These discussions emerged as a number of participants from this group had a shared experience of encountering someone whose presentation of gender did not follow the discursively dominant binary. Unlike with Troy, above, they spoke of the case with confusion but respect.

Flora:	Wasn't there that boy [redacted] in year seven …
Erica:	Everyone thought he was a girl!
Reuben:	He was wasn't it?
Pedro:	[quietly] He is, or she is, he went to my old school.
Flora:	Apparently he was a girl, but he told everyone he was a boy, no one knew.
Reuben:	Because when all the girls went to have their shots he went as well.
Flora:	Yeah the HPV jab.
Erica:	[gasps] I didn't know that, I thought he was actually a boy but everyone thought he was a girl.
Pedro:	Yeah coz on the register it said- …
Flora:	Female.
Pedro:	[redacted]

Erica: I think he's gone now...
Flora: ... yeah they've gone.
Pedro: They have gone.
Reuben: On the register it was a girl's name, but he liked to be called a boy's name...
Pedro: ... the boy's version and he said his mum made a mistake.
Flora: Yeah like it was his sister's name, but no one knew, it was really weird.

(City High, Group One, Session Four)

The general tone of the conversation was one of respect, and the participants' willingness to work around preferred pronouns also shows an openness to the individual's gender expression. However, the conversation also revealed that the cohort more widely struggled with the non-cisnormative presentation of gender. Pedro explained that the person had 'gone now', emphasising the word *gone*. This indicates that their presentation of gender was not reconcilable with the hyper-regulatory space of the school and in this instance led to the individual leaving. This reminds all of those who were present during his time at school and his subsequent leaving of the potential outcomes associated with non-cisnormative gender presentation.

The Persistence of the Gender Binary and its Knowability

Participants generally believed that an individual is either male *or* female and that this should be evident and attributable in interaction. This further limits the extent to which gender can be understood as a troubled category in youth despite knowledge of gender beyond the binary being evident. For example, when discussing the inbetweener, Leticia commented 'but surely you'd know if it was a boy or a girl if you were talking to them' (City High, Group One, Session Four). Furthermore, in Group Two at City High Lauren was desperate to know the 'actual' gender of the respondent, further indicating that that there is a desire for gender to be a stable and attributable element of one's identity. Such moments paint a picture of the 'ontological security' provided by gender in young people's increasingly insecure worlds (Nayak and Kehily 2008: 198) and further highlight

What is Gender?

the 'unending desire to know the truth of sex categories'. (Nayak and Kehily 2008: 166)

Young people see gender as a binary in terms of biology, and because they expect to 'discover' this gender through interaction articulations of taste can be a way of either affirming or troubling the gender identity that one presents and/or is read as. The potential for shunning or mockery that is experienced in the hyper-regulatory space of high school (see Chapter 2) therefore helps us to understand why there may be motivation to articulate tastes that are coherent with the gender attributed, as a means of 'fitting in'. Gender therefore matters in youth taste cultures, and this was discussed by participants at City High:

Pedro: Coz if it was a boy they'd want to be [.] they don't want to [.] portray themselves as feminine.
Flora: It's alright for a girl to be tom boyish but not so much for a boy to be like a girl.
[Erica nods]
Erica: If a boy says anything a bit like a girl they'll call them gay.
Flora: ... gay.
Leticia: That's because society.

(City High, Group Two, Session Four)

This illustrates that the ways in which gender is presented *matters*, as discourses of gender appropriateness *regulate*. For example, Pedro and Flora show that it would be problematic to be attributed as male but to 'portray as feminine'. This leads me to my final area of discussion in relation to young people's understandings of gender, the conflation of gender and sexuality. This is a potentially highly regulatory factor in gender expression under patriarchy in the hyper-regulatory space of high school.

Conflating Sexuality with Gender

'It's either a girl or gay' (Melark, Girls High, Session One)

When participants discussed non-binary gender identities they tended to conflate gender identity with sexual orientation. This was particularly pronounced with boys and/or masculinity and can therefore help to explain boys' motivation to articulate gender appropriate taste within a patriarchal context (see following chapter). For example, at Girls High Melark talks about one of the prompt-writers, stating 'it's either a girl or gay' (Session One). Melark was not 'corrected' and told that gay is not a gender, which is a departure from what I observed in other groups when similar comments were made. For example, when discussing the potential genders of the prompt-writers, the following conversation took place:

> Phoebe: I didn't think inbetween was good, I needed a gay one.
> Interviewer: What's the difference? How does gay?
> Phoebe: Well because if you're gay you're not –
> Sara: – it's not a gender is it!
> [Rachel and Juan laugh]
> Phoebe: [laughing] No I'm not saying that but like, if they're inbetween they probably think like, oh I dunno [puts head into arms that are folded up on the desk and then raises her head again] erm, I dunno I just needed that.
> (City High, Group Two, Session Four)

In this conversation we see that for Phoebe, the term 'gay' would have better conceptualised a transgressive gender identity. However, this is picked up by Sara (who has previously critiqued conventional conceptions of gender). The playful manner in which Sara 'corrects' Phoebe is less threatening than a stern telling off, but she is nevertheless successful in informing Phoebe that she is 'wrong' to conceive of gay as a gender identity. However, in this conversation we see Phoebe struggling to articulate her own understandings of gender. By understanding some gender practices as *gay* gender practices, we can better make sense of how this may be problematic for young people under patriarchy (especially boys). Additionally, it is worth noting that it was almost always the word 'gay' that was conflated with a gender identity and not lesbian (or other sexual orientations). In the instances when participants such as Mary and Phoebe discussed having been called a lesbian they suggested that while it may have been intended as an insult, it was not usually conflated with a gender identity as was the case with the word gay. When participants discussed this distinction they described how the word gay was more harmful (and thus regulatory) for boys than the word lesbian was for girls. For example, on two occasions Sara said, 'it doesn't affect girls as much'. This connects to the work of Nayak and Kehily who found that the term lesbian was used 'by young men as a vernacular form of abuse' (2008: 162) against girls. However, they also found that girls subject to these forms of abuse would often 'overturn the sign value' of such insults by enacting forms of lesbianism (2008: 162). Of course I am keen to emphasise that this is what participants described as being the case, and it does not take into account the lived realities, stresses and symbolic violence faced by those labelled lesbian in a heteronormative (patriarchal) context.

This conflation of gender and sexuality matters because it demonstrates young people's difficulties in thinking of gender outside of the binary. If young people conflate gender inappropriate taste with a minority sexuality, then this is problematic for the individual within a heteronormative context under patriarchy. There is motivation then for young people, especially boys, to articulate tastes that are coherent with the gender that they present as.

Concluding Remarks

In the focus groups a number of participants gave accounts of gender which offered space for young people to perform versions of gender that may not fit with what is 'conventional'. However, in almost all accounts it was suggested that ultimately, 'underneath' a person's performance, one is always male *or* female, never both or neither. And thus, despite personal experiences, popular cultural representations and educational lessons on gender beyond the cisnormative binary, the vast majority of young people seem invested in the gender binary and the discoverability of a fixed gender. Of the conversations that I observed there was some sense of gender from a queer perspective, whereby young people could imagine some form of gender fluidity. However, this was very rarely something that the participants had actually experienced. This demonstrates the disjuncture between the advancement of queer theory and the lived experiences of young people, where flippant comments reinforced discourses of gender appropriateness. And so what this chapter demonstrates is that while understood as a social group where 'identity and status are questioned, suspended or reversed' (Hesmondhalgh 2005: 37), young people overwhelmingly (re)produce dominant discourses rather than transgressing them when it comes to gender.

I think it is fair to say that increasing representation of non-cisnormative gender identities in popular culture will start to have an impact on how people of all ages come to understand the fluidity of gender. Discussions in the focus groups here demonstrate the important role that characters such as Unique on *Glee* (Fox 2009–15) play in opening up gender to young people and providing a point of reference to help them to frame and develop their understanding. But as the discussions at Outskirts High show, these media representations need to be placed alongside comprehensive sex and sexuality education for young people. Non-cisnormative genders were routinely rendered 'weird' by young people, discursively reproducing queer, trans and non-binary youth as 'Other' – a label not to be taken lightly in the hyper-regulatory space of high school where being shunned is a very real possibility. Furthermore, the conflation that has been made between gender and sexuality can be seen to play a particularly important role in the lives of boys. If feminine tastes render the boys that express them 'gay' then this is potentially highly problematic for boys seeking to perform hegemonic masculinity under patriarchy. As I show in the chapters that follow, the ideas about gender that young people express have a profound impact on how they experience taste and talk about the things it is appropriate for them to say they like.

4

Boys Like This: Masculinity and Appropriate Tastes for Boys

> 'I'm not being sexist or stereotyping, but I think boys more prefer the action'
>
> (Joe, City High, Group One, Session Two)
>
> 'If he came round my house brandishing a copy of Twilight I'd punch him'
>
> (Troy, Outskirts High, Session Three)

People in the West are worried about boys, who have been described as both *'at risk* and also *a risk to others'* (Roberts 2014: 3, emphasis in original). Cultural commentators, news anchors, politicians and academics articulate concerns and anxieties about the under-achievement of boys; about the high suicide levels of young men; about the increasing levels of white male violence (at both mass and domestic levels). Jennifer Siebel Newsom's documentary *The Mask You Live In* (2015) has revealed the ways in which boys and young men suffer emotionally when trying to perform and identify with narrow definitions of masculinity in the USA. Meanwhile, the resurgence of right wing politics across the neoliberal West has lamented the rise of feminists and liberals emasculating 'our boys' and ever increasingly we are seeing an amplified identification with traditional gender roles amid increasing fascist rhetoric. The 2014 suicide of Robin

Williams led to an international conversation about men's mental health, and the reluctance of men and boys to talk about how they're feeling. These are big issues and are ones that are taken seriously by feminists who have the aim of achieving gender equality, concerned that no person is limited by gendered norms.

In this chapter I explore the ways in which masculinity is reproduced in everyday contexts, demonstrating that mundane conversations about taste and culture feed into wider discourses of what it means 'to be a man'. Thus, while masculinity may be discursively reproduced and arbitrarily attached to boys' bodies, it is nevertheless made 'real' within interactions. I show here that boys are much more limited than girls in what they feel comfortable saying they like, and that fear of homosexualisation continues to regulate boys' articulations of taste. I discuss how boys align themselves with cultural texts which foreground physicality, be that through watching sports such as football, or listening to music that demonstrates technical skills, such as guitar bands. I also show how boys simultaneously reject feminine cultural texts in the process. Given the findings discussed in this chapter it is perhaps not surprising that I suggest that we should continue to worry for boys and their future(s).

Theorising Masculinity and Boyhood(s): The Background

The current theoretical context around masculinities is shifting. Steve Roberts has claimed that the 'shifting and complex nature of masculinity as a gender category belies and unsettles fixed normative definitions of masculinity' (2014: 4). As such, the academic field surrounding young masculinities has splintered, with the new kids on the block, proponents of 'inclusive masculinity theory' (Anderson 2009; McCormack 2012), asking serious questions of the more established theory of 'hegemonic masculinity' (developed by Connell 1995). Within the British context, Ingram and Waller (2014) have noted that the forms of masculinity expressed within the contemporary context are 'undeniably different' from those of the 1970s and 1980s, but have nevertheless remained less optimistic about what this means for the inclusivity of masculinity. Ingram and Waller choose to describe these shifts as 'a repackaging of forms of domination' (2014: 39) rather than as a softening of it. For those unfamiliar with the complex terrain of masculinity theory, it would be useful for me to provide an overview of this shifting academic field.

Hegemonic Masculinity Theory

Raewyn Connell's theory of hegemonic masculinity uses Gramsci's concept of hegemony as a means of understanding how a particular form of masculinity is able to guarantee the dominant position of (particular types of) men (Connell 2005: 77). Because of its use of hegemony, the concept has been appealing to many researching in this field. What makes the theory of hegemonic masculinity so attractive is the way in which it illuminates the breadth of masculinities available to individuals, whilst also acknowledging that not all of these masculinities are equal. Hegemonic masculinity theory de-essentialises masculine behaviour, seeing it as a construction rather than an immutable 'fact'. This also helps to make sense of how 'traditionally masculine' stereotypes are discursively (re)produced by young people. Lusher and Robins contribute to this understanding, suggesting that hegemonic masculinity provides a prototype for 'enabling people to act certain ways' (2009: 369), helping us to develop an understanding of how these discourses (re)produce gender through embodied performance.

What makes masculinities *hegemonic* rather than simply *multiple* is the hierarchy that is (re)produced. Masculinity and hierarchy can be usefully understood through the concept of hegemony: 'hegemony in the gender order is the use of culture for such disciplinary purposes: setting standards, claiming popular assent and discrediting those that fall short' (Connell 2005: 214). Through the application of hegemony we can start to see how some versions of masculinity are privileged within contemporary culture. However, Connell also defines masculinity in a way that helps us to understand the relationship it has to femininity in terms of domination:

> Hegemonic masculinity can be defined as the configuration of gender practice which embodies the currently accepted answer to the problem of the legitimacy of patriarchy, which guarantees (or is taken to guarantee) the dominant position of men and the subordination of women.
>
> (Connell 2005: 77)

As I show in this and the following chapter, the routine rejection of femininity for both boys and girls is one such way in which the patriarchy is legitimised. The concept of hegemonic masculinity therefore helps us to understand the motivations behind (re)producing masculinity in 'traditional' ways, as from this theoretical perspective to not conform or to reject the currently accepted 'ideal' is to almost certainly be placed in a position of subordination within the wider gender 'order'. That said, Connell herself also argues that 'this is not to say that the most visible bearers of hegemonic masculinity are always the most powerful people' (2005: 77), forcing us to undertake a close reading of how masculinity is understood and (re)produced in each context. Furthermore, the concept becomes a little cumbersome when applied to boys and men of colour, who find themselves disadvantaged by the racist discourses that negatively intersect with what would otherwise be the privileges of inhabiting masculine subjectivities.

As I show in this chapter, context is crucial to how young people's tastes are gendered, and ultimately rendered appropriate or not. Such approaches to masculinity therefore help us to make sense of how discourses of traditional masculinities have remained pervasive in terms of 'the current ideal' (Cheng 1999: 297).

Inclusive Masculinity Theory

To answer the question of 'does hegemonic masculinity theory work?' with 'sometimes' might make it appear that I am sitting on the fence. But this is not the case at all; rather I believe that to say 'sometimes' is to acknowledge the complexities of masculinity within the context of contemporary youth taste culture(s); perhaps indeed *especially* within the context of contemporary youth taste cultures. In reflecting on some of the limitations of hegemonic masculinity theory it would therefore be useful to outline critiques and theories posited as alternatives.

The development of inclusive masculinity theory has raised questions with respect to many of the assumptions made within the hegemonic masculinity school of thought. Some of the main criticisms of Connell's hegemonic masculinity theory are that her focus is too simplistic, and that the theory does not account for the contradictory ways in which individuals engage with masculinity (Wetherell and Edley 1999). I would

Masculinity and Appropriate Tastes for Boys

add to this critique that it does not account for the contradictory ways in which female, queer and non-binary individuals engage with these masculinities either (as well as people of colour and disabled folk). A number of other theorists have suggested that researchers have become over-reliant on Connell's theory of hegemonic masculinity, overlooking the complexities of masculinity in their search for hegemony (Anderson 2009; McCormack 2012; Pringle 2005). Of the critiques of Connell's theory of hegemonic masculinity, inclusive masculinity is one that has gained traction in recent years, with the key thinkers postulating this theory being Eric Anderson (2009) and Mark McCormack (2012).

Within Anderson's inclusive masculinity theory an understanding is developed where masculinity is not maintained within a hierarchical (and thus oppressive) hegemony. Instead, proponents of inclusive masculinity theory argue that 'many archetypes of masculinity can be socially esteemed' (McCormack 2012: 45). Following on from this, McCormack argues that 'there will be a marked expansion in the range of permissible behaviours for boys and men' (2012: 45). Without fear of being homosexualised it is claimed that boys can 'act in ways once considered transgressive without the threat of homophobic policing' (McCormack 2012: 45). This is because it is argued that cultural homophobia is less regulative within the contemporary British context. The most significant challenge to hegemonic masculinity theory offered by inclusive masculinity theory is therefore in the questioning of the heterosexuality that is assumed to be privileged within the hegemonic masculine hierarchy. Anderson believes that hegemonic, traditional (or to use Anderson's term 'orthodox') forms of masculinity only occur pervasively in contexts of what he terms 'homohysteria', described by McCormack as 'the cultural fear of being homosexualised' (2012: 44). During periods of homohysteria, Anderson argues that men need to 'publicly align their social identities with heterosexuality in order to avoid homosexual suspicion' (2009: 8). Therefore within inclusive masculinity theory it is argued that 'there is an awareness that heterosexual men can act in ways once associated with homosexuality, with less threat to their public identity has heterosexual' (McCormack 2012: 7). This means that in periods of diminished homohysteria, homophobia would be unable to regulate masculinity in the ways that Connell's theory of hegemonic masculinity allows for.

Inclusive masculinity theorists are keen to assert that we do not live in a gender utopia (Anderson 2009: 14), but are nevertheless optimistic about the future. McCormack, for example, draws on empirical evidence in his claim that 'boys ascribing to masculine archetypes can still maintain high school status' (McCormack 2012: xxviii). Here, he emphasises that in some instances phrases such as 'that's so gay' are not necessarily homophobic, and thus argues that cultural context is crucial to how we understand these words as scholars (2012: 118). If this is the case, there are potentially wide-ranging effects on how we understand contemporary boy culture(s), especially in terms of hegemonic masculinity. I follow McCormack's thesis that context is indeed key, but as I demonstrate in this research we should proceed cautiously in understanding the role of homophobia in young people's lives – things are certainly getting better but, as Ingram and Waller (2014) have noted, we should not throw 'the baby out with the bathwater' when offering alternatives to Connell's theory of hegemonic masculinity theory.

Theorising and Understanding Boy Cultures: What We Know

In terms of hegemonic masculinity, we can begin to understand some of the ways in which discourses of boys' physicality have led to a problematic over-emphasis on the deviant nature of youth masculinities. Meanwhile inclusive masculinity proposes that there is no one dominant form of masculinity, that all can be valued. But boyhood is a particularly unique time for those analysing masculinities, as this is a time when people are 'becoming more aware of their gender roles and what is socially appropriate for a male or a female' (Dumais 2002: 59).

Nayak and Kehily refer to boys as 'in crisis', as a result of shifting gender norms in late-modernity (2008: 42). Barker connects 'the crisis of masculinity' directly to the lives of young men, arguing that the ways in which men and boys are socialised have led to the high death rates amongst this social group: 'they are trying to live up to certain models of manhood – they are dying to prove that they are "real men"' (2005: 2). Barker's argument starkly demonstrates the need for us to interrogate the discourses of masculinity that young people (re)produce. Despite the

Masculinity and Appropriate Tastes for Boys

arbitrariness of masculinity, Barker's comments reveal the very real lived consequences of masculinity experienced by boys across the world – and this emphasises the need for feminist intervention.

In terms of crime and deviance, sociologists such as Andersson (2008) have stressed that young males are seen as a deviant group within society. Related to this, Robb has noted that the discourses of violence and masculinity that are regularly (re)produced and (re)presented within contemporary culture have had an impact on the realities of boys living today, arguing that they are 'only too aware of the negative ways in which boys and men are represented in the mass media and elsewhere' (2007: 120). Frosh, Phoenix and Pattman have also found instances of deviance in their work, finding that 'popular masculinity involves "hardness", sporting prowess, "coolness", casual treatment of homework and being adept at "cussing"' (2002: 10). This is something which holds particular significance for Britain's black youth.

Studies into boy cultures and youth masculinities have also highlighted the centrality of compulsory heterosexuality and the regulatory presence of homophobia. The range of studies, including this book, that have identified discourses of homophobia within contemporary boy culture(s) render it worthy of discussion despite its critiques from proponents of inclusive masculinity theory. Sexuality is an important factor in how gender is experienced and (re)produced for those who present as boys, in particular due to the fragility of masculinity within a hegemonic framework. A wide range of studies have found that homosexuality is routinely rejected in boys' cultures (Epstein and Johnson 1998; Frosh, Phoenix and Pattman 2002; Nayak and Kehily 1996; Rasmussen 2004). When we compare this to studies of girls in the UK, where some studies have noted how girls enact lesbian displays as forms of resistance (Blackman 1998; Nayak and Kehily 2008), we can see that the experiences of boys and girls are markedly different (let alone those who live outside the gender binary). Homophobia has thus been discussed as playing a central role in the discursive regulation and (re)production of youth masculinities within a hegemonic framework.

In terms of boys as audiences of popular culture, Debbie Ging has found that these discourses of 'traditional' masculinity can be observed in boys' media usage, whereby boys 'actively perform media usage as a means of affirming and, in some cases, policing masculinity' (2005: 45). In this affirmation and/or policing of masculinity, Ging (2005) found that boys would align themselves with texts that signified acceptable codes of masculinity while also distancing themselves from texts considered to be feminine. Within Ging's (2005) observations, a (hegemonic) hierarchy of masculinity that rendered some forms of cultural preference acceptable and others inappropriate was key, further highlighting the heuristic applicability of Connell's theory of hegemonic masculinity. Ging believed that the motivation to conform was located within the fear of homosexualisation, with homophobic remarks being used as a means of policing boys at different levels (2005: 46), something that was very familiar to the boys' experiences outlined in this book.

There is debate within the academic field as to whether or not boys are even 'in-crisis' and this is an important question to ponder for all youth and childhood researchers. Steve Roberts (2014) has suggested that there is nothing particularly new about the claim that masculinity is in crisis, arguing that this concept emerged as far back as the 1800s. Furthermore, there are legitimate concerns that the panics about boys being in crisis ignore intersections of class, race and ability which often have a much bigger impact on boys' attainment than their gender alone (Ashley 2009; Roberts 2012).

In this and the chapter that follows, I show that tastes which are appropriate for boys are much more limited than those deemed appropriate for girls. Part of this is as a result of the devaluation of the feminine, which fits theoretical assumptions of gendered value (see Paechter 2006). I also demonstrate that the limits of appropriate tastes for boys are bound up with the power that is associated with masculinity, and I show that cultural texts are inscribed with masculine value. With respect to this aspect we see the usefulness of Connell's (1995) theory of hegemonic masculinity as it allows us to make sense of the pervasiveness of 'traditionally' masculine stereotypes. However, what I did not find was the admiration of the hegemonic masculine 'prototypes' that has often been associated with hegemonic masculinity. This was exemplified by the problematisation of the tastes of one of the prompt-writers who was deemed *too* masculine, whose highly stereotypical tastes were problematised and ridiculed by the participants (subject of further discussion in Chapter 6). However, just because some of the more stereotypical versions of masculinity were problematised by participants (male and female), this does not mean that I found inclusive masculinity to be in operation. As I further explore in this chapter, fear of homosexualistion remained regulatory for the boys in this study.

Boys' Tastes, Masculinity and the Identity Pages

Results from the identity pages (outlined in Chapter 1) showed that boys mentioned a narrower range of texts than girls in their taste articulations. Broadly speaking, boys tended to express preferences for sports-based texts and an aversion for romance texts (which followed Bennett et al.'s (2005: 10) findings with respect to adult men). Commonly mentioned preferences included programmes and channels such as *Match of the Day* (BBC 1964 – present), *Sky Sports*, and *Bundesliga*. Footballers also featured in the celebrities boys said they liked such as Russell Martin, Zak Whitbread, Marc Tierney, Andrew Surman, Wes Hoolahan, Grant Holt, Simeon Jackson and Lionel Messi. In terms of romance films (deemed feminine), boys rarely included titles, opting instead to reject the genre as a whole. Given the genre's association with female audiences (Radway 1987), it is perhaps not all that surprising that boys are distancing themselves from such films. However, as I show in the following chapter, respondents who described themselves as female tended to articulate a wider range of texts (in both their likes and dislikes), suggesting distinct gendered experiences of taste during youth.

Generally speaking, demarcation of taste along gender lines was not particularly evident on the identity pages, with a number of texts featuring in responses along the gender spectrum. For example, comedy films and texts such as the film *Kidulthood* (2006), television programmes such as *Friends* (NBC 1994–2004), *Doctor Who* (BBC 1963–89; 2005– present) and *Britain's Got Talent* (ITV 2007–present) and musical genres such as RnB featured on the pages of young people of different genders. Such a broad range of responses problematised attempts to analyse patterns of taste, but did illuminate the diversity of tastes within the sample group. However, when prompts demonstrating such diversity were given to the focus group participants, the gendered value of particular texts were discussed, revealing the nuanced understanding young people have of gendered value and appropriateness of cultural texts. Through these discussions, notions of gender appropriate or inappropriate taste were at the forefront, allowing us to see how the inscription of gender into cultural texts impacts how gender is discursively (re)produced. What I found to be particularly interesting was that not only did participants use femininity as a tool in their sense-making of masculinity, but also that girls played an important part in the discursive (re)production of masculinity too. This demonstrates the usefulness of undertaking empirical youth research which engages with young people of more than just one gender. One of the main ways in which texts were rendered appropriate for boys was if they held masculine value. Texts that held masculine value were considered appropriate for boys to like, and allowed for the (re)production of the dominant discourses of gender.

Masculine Value

Masculine value is held by texts that are seen to be of particular importance or significance to male audiences. Texts are not inherently valuable on the grounds of gender, but rather this value is inscribed into texts by audience members (in this case, the young people that took part in this study). Thinking about texts as having some gendered value helps us to make sense of how gender is discursively (re)produced in contemporary youth taste cultures. In particular, it reminds us of the role that everyday engagement of popular culture plays in the (re)production of identity.

Gender appropriateness matters because young people largely conceive of gender in the binary, and as I show in this chapter not conforming to the 'right side' of the binary in gender expressions can lead to problematisation of the individual's tastes. This problematisation – as discussed in Chapter 2 – is to be avoided as it routinely takes the form of 'shunning' – something that I have shown young people do not want to be subject to in the hyper-regulatory space of the high school. Understanding what has masculine value is thus of importance to boys, as one would be able to (re)produce a socially acceptable version of masculinity by aligning himself with texts that are collectively understood to be 'for boys' and thus masculine. If we think of this in terms of McCormack's metaphor of 'masculine capital' then boys would be able to 'buy immunity from stigma' (McCormack 2012: 50) by aligning themselves with texts that have masculine value and distancing themselves by saying they dislike texts that have feminine value.[1] This allows a boy to present a (cis)male identity that is read as discursively appropriate. Boys' gender appropriate taste is therefore not only about recognising and responding appropriately to cultural texts that hold masculine value, but also about rejecting the feminine. This follows existing work in the field such as that by Debbie Ging, who showed that problematic texts (such as feminine ones) 'did not function as "affirmation texts", outside of providing boys with an opportunity to perform – sometimes in highly exaggerated ways – their dislike of the texts' (2005: 46). As I showed with the quote which opened this chapter, texts seen to hold feminine value, such as the film *Twilight* (2008), provided moments where this appropriate masculine rejection of the feminine could be performed. As I demonstrate in the data presented below, properties of hegemonic masculinity (physicality and compulsory (hetero)sexuality) were placed centrally with respect to the tastes of boys.

Boys Like: Texts that Foreground Physicality

'Masculine' tastes were observed in the articulation made by boys and girls in the focus groups, showing some of the more transgressive elements of girls' tastes as compared to boys. The texts that the participants discussed as being valuable in terms of masculinity very clearly featured the properties of hegemonic masculinity, such as physical strength (Connell 2005), as well as 'domination, aggressiveness, competitiveness, athletic prowess, stoicism and control' (Cheng 1999: 298). The texts than can allow for these properties to be read into them therefore play an important role in the perceptions and performances of boys' tastes.

Boys Like: Violence, Conflict and Action

Properties of hegemonic masculinity such as aggression and violence (Cheng 1999: 298) played an important role in how participants talked about the gender appropriateness of cultural texts that portrayed violence. Past studies have indicated that texts from horror and action genres were found to have significance for boys (Ging 2005: 33), and so the pervasiveness of these discourses is notable. Television programmes such as *The Walking Dead* (AMC 2010–present), *Game of Thrones* (HBO 2011–present), *Breaking Bad* (AMC 2008–13), and celebrities such as

Girls Like This, Boys Like That

Chuck Norris were discussed as playing central roles in boys' daily discussions about media and culture. Troy relayed a common style of conversation he has with his friends about *The Walking Dead*: 'and everyone like after every episode we were like *did you see when that dude totally got the axe in the face* and everyone was like that was so good!' (Outskirts High, Session Three)

In discussing the tastes of one prompt-writer, City High participant Joe draws on all of the texts that he sees as having masculine value in action and conflict, and explicates their connection to masculinity:

> He kind of likes a bit of action, I mean Doctor Who, obviously I wouldn't say it's massively action packed, but there's like guns and stuff, and then like the celebrities, yeah well they are conflicty, and erm, Avatar, that's kind of about war and yeah. So yeah obviously, and, yeah [...] yeah. Conflict, violence, action.
>
> (Joe, City High, Group One, Session Two)

By summing up at the end, 'conflict, violence, action', Joe reinforces his understanding of the texts holding masculine value by associating them 'obviously' to a 'he'. In this statement Joe also discussed some of the texts that hold these properties in his opinion, but that may be less obviously 'masculine', such as *Doctor Who* (BBC 1963–89, 2005–present). When he discusses *Doctor Who* he describes it as 'not massively action packed' (and thus not *too* masculine), but by mentioning 'guns and stuff' (signifiers of violence) he is nevertheless able to inscribe it with masculine value, rendering it appropriate for boys to like.

Horror was another area where participants drew on the collective understanding of violence and conflict as being imbued with masculine value. Horror was a genre that was seen to have masculine value on the whole, but, as I demonstrate in the following chapter, was not something that only boys engaged with. For example, Sara noted that, 'boys and girls do like horror but boys do prefer them' (City High, Group Two, Session Two). However, this perception is complicated by her friend Lauren who considers the intersections of age and gender, commenting that 'older teenagers that are girls, like horrors, but most [boys] like, from a younger teenage kind of age like horrors, so it's more about age' (City High, Group Two, Session Two). This may offer an understanding of how it is that boys are understood to more inherently like horrors, while girls grow to like

Masculinity and Appropriate Tastes for Boys

them over time. This is not to say that there aren't boys that don't like horror – as with other texts that have masculine value – but rather that within these spaces this is not something that was expressed, and thus the discursive association between the horror genre and boys was (re)produced. For example, when Leticia emphasises 'stereotypically' in the statement 'most boys, *stereotypically*, most boys think horror is amazing' (City High, Group One, Session Four) she shows that she doesn't necessarily believe the association between horror and boys to be an essential one.

In the discussions there was very little justification given by participants as to why they believed that horror had masculine value. But in conversations where representations of death were shown, a glimpse into the connections between boys and violence can be seen. For example, in a discussion about the film *Titanic* (1997), a distinction is made between styles of death and the gender of the audience it appeals to:

Phoebe:	Because it's romance, but then there's like ultimate death in it so.
Interviewer:	Ultimate death.
Phoebe:	Yeah people die and get a bit of love in it too.
Mary:	Yeah but that's the kind of death films that girls like.
Rachel:	Yeah but its sad death it's like emotional death isn't it not gruesome death, like blood and gore and that.
Lauren:	It's not like [in gruff voice] give me your money or I'm gonna finish you!
Juan:	Yeah but people die in Disney films for god sake so.
	(City High, Group Two, Session Four)

Gendered readings are observable across this dialogue. Phoebe reads the romance in *Titanic* as having feminine value (an area to which I turn in the following chapter), while her peers did not see the presence of death within the film as able to supersede the overwhelming femininity of the text as a whole. The way in which death is represented in films therefore plays a role in the gendered value that a text is seen to hold. For example, Rachel says that the death in *Titanic* is not masculine because it is not 'gruesome' and doesn't involve 'gore', and Lauren says that it needs to be violent in some way in order to be masculine (seen in her imitation of a gangster). Meanwhile, Juan uses the example of (childish and feminine) Disney to

85

make the case that not all death can be understood in (essentially) masculine terms. The above conversation also shows that the gendering of texts is nuanced and complicated, and that young people are nevertheless sophisticated meaning makers when it comes to understanding how and/ or why some texts hold forms of gendered value. Through the emphasis on blood and gore we can again see the connection between the properties of hegemonic masculinity and the texts inscribed with masculine value. Given the anxieties that we see expressed about boys in terms of violence it is particularly noteworthy that both boys and girls (re)produce these narratives in their discussions of texts that are deemed appropriate for boys to like. Sport offers a different form of action that is understood as appropriate for boys to like.

Boys Like: Sport

> 'You kind of say you're into sport it kind of shows you as yeah as kind of what boys do.'
> (Joe, City High, Group One, Session Three)

As also seen in the wider academic field (Anderson 2009; Gilbert and Gilbert 1998; Messner 1992; Renold 1997; Swain 2000), sport played a central role in the discussions that participants had about boys' tastes. Discussions included ideas about the practice of sport as well as the consumption of sport as being appropriate for boys. The emphasis on physicality and competitiveness can help us to understand how a particular version of masculinity is evoked when participants discuss sport as being appropriate for boys to like. In the majority of the conversations about sport, it was football (soccer) in particular that was seen as central to boys' tastes and wider cultural lives. There was a general assumption across the groups that 'sport' was valuable in terms of masculinity, with a range of statements being made that liking sport is what boys 'do'. In one session football was described as 'must watch' for boys so that they could talk about it the following day. Anna said that 'boys worship football' (Outskirts High, Session One) and in the same session Katherine said 'boys like, try to like sports to look cool', while in a different group Josh commented that 'the general topic for boys is like they talk about football or games and stuff [...] like if it had football on there I'd automatically think it was a boy' (City High, Group Two, Session One).

Masculinity and Appropriate Tastes for Boys

In making sense of why it was that sport was so central to boys' tastes, Joe thoughtfully drew upon the properties of hegemonic masculinity, demonstrating why sport has masculine value:

> Joe: For a guy you'd talk about sport because erm I think like sport kind of is something related to like power and like masculinity so if you kind of say you're into sport it kind of shows you as yeah as kind of what boys do.
>
> (City High, Group One, Session Three)

Joe shows *how* and *why* he thinks sport is connected to masculinity, mirroring how sport and 'macho versions of masculinity' (McCormack 2011: 86) have been conceptualised within academic theory. In Joe's deconstruction of boys' tastes and masculinity we can see his acknowledgement that these hegemonic properties are not inherent within the text but nevertheless hold value for boys. Such connections should not be overstated, as they are alluded to rather than directly discussed, but do reflect a much wider awareness of gender stereotypes that young people have. As I will argue in the concluding chapter of this book, this is important as it shows potential for considerable gender reflexivity during youth, and thus there is potential for change in young people's experiences of gender – including the acceptance of non-normative gender(s).

As sport recurred as an important text for boys in both the identity pages and the initial focus groups, I asked participants questions that I hoped would reveal more about the role that boys' preference for sport played in their everyday experiences. It was here that I learned that while it was appropriate for boys to articulate a preference for sports, they did not need to articulate much knowledge about sport to 'prove' their taste – largely because this knowledge was assumed on account of them presenting as male. What was noteworthy in these conversations was that although there was a perception that 'boys like football', this was not always experienced in 'real life'. Group member Naomi[2] felt that although boys might *say* they like football, she found that they didn't always engage with football in a way that reflected this. Naomi and her friends reflect on this in relation to their own experiences:

> Naomi: I ask the boys and they say they haven't watched it and I've watched all the games and that's really weird for me 'cause I watch all the Euro matches.

Phoebe: A lot of boys haven't watched the matches.
Interviewer: What makes that weird do you think?
Naomi: Because none of the boys wa-tched it! And so.
Mary: And you'd stereotypically think –
Sara: –you'd expect to have a conversation with a boy about it.

(City High, Group Two, Session One)

Much of this conversation shows Naomi claiming masculine taste, an area to which I return in my discussion of girls and transgressive tastes, but it also illuminates that while football may hold masculine value and be an appropriate taste for boys to articulate, these boys do not necessarily exhibit much more than a basic articulation of preference on a day-to-day basis. We nevertheless see boys tied to football, as shown in Naomi's use of the word weird, indicating that she would otherwise *expect* to find boys invested in sports in the same way that she is. While there is awareness that these associations are constructed, with the use of phrases such as 'you'd stereotypically think', the discursive association between boys, sport and masculinity are nevertheless (re)produced. As the conversation continued the group members worked through strategies that would allow Naomi's experiences to make sense in relation to the dominant discourses of masculinity. Emphasis in these cases is placed upon the specificities of boys' engagement with sport, where the discussion centred on the importance of *teams* to boys, rather than simply everything to do with football.

Phoebe: But I think a lot of boys like certain teams.
Josh: Yeah boys support certain teams.
Juan: Yeah.
Sara: Yeah they don't watch all –
Josh: –I support one team, I'll only watch their matches unless it was a really good match.

(City High, Group Two, Session One)

By emphasising that it would be unrealistic for boys to watch *all* of the football matches that were shown and that it would be a specific team that would be followed instead, the discourse of 'boys like football' is not problematised in these accounts. We also see that Josh acts as 'expert' in providing an explanation from a boy's perspective – something that boys did often within the focus groups. The masculine value of football is therefore (re)produced despite Naomi's valid experiences to the contrary, and so the potential challenge to the dominant discourses is minimised.

The prevalence of sport within boys' taste cultures leads us to ask what might happen should a boy not be openly interested in watching and/or playing sport. When I asked the participants to reflect on what they felt the outcomes of such articulations were, Phoebe thought that some boys simply would not make it known that they did not like sport, saying *'that's just common knowledge not to'* (City High, Group Two, Session One). Looking back at the chapter which discussed hyper-regulation during youth (Chapter 2) it is likely the case that a boy may be concerned that he would be shunned for his preferences. For boys such as this, who do not like sport, I found that one way of combatting the potential of shunning would be to articulate a preference for a different text that held masculine value – importantly a text that also foregrounded physicality.

The need to 'be into something else' was described as key by participants from Group Two at City High and alluded to by other groups. Music was seen to be an important area that had the potential to hold masculine value that could balance a boy's dislike for sport. However, it was not simply *all* music that was understood to have masculine value, but music that demonstrated technical skill which was considered appropriate for boys to like (something I also witnessed in the exploratory ethnography). Technical skill then, which is located in the physical skill needed to be able to play musical instruments, follows theorisations by Connell and Messerschmidt who argued that 'in youth, skilled bodily activity becomes a prime indicator of masculinity' (2005: 851).

Boys Like: Music with Instruments

> 'The people I know what don't like sport are more into their music'.
> (Juan, City High, Group Two, Session One)

Instruments in music play an important role in understanding where the masculine value of music is held as this allows boys to articulate preference for acts demonstrating technical ability – in much the same way that footballers do. Josh makes this distinction in his discussion of The Beatles, who, he said, despite having the potential to be perceived as a boyband, were certainly not problematic for boys to like:

> It's good music like, I sort of think more on the instrument kind of side, I don't like pop because it's mainly singing but I like The Beatles because they have good guitar and pianos and I don't really think it's about the boyband sort of view, the sort of singing I don't like the whole.
>
> (Josh, City High, Group Two, Session One)

Through the use of instruments the artist is able to demonstrate their 'authenticity' in musicality, which has been found to have a high premium for school-age audiences (Ashley 2011). So while pop acts such as One Direction, Justin Bieber and The Jonas Brothers were considered inappropriate for boys to like, rock and metal acts such as Linkin Park, Snow Patrol and Frank Turner all featured within the study. Joe draws out the skills involved in playing music as being central to why boys are interested in particular forms of music:

> I think girls care more about, as you [previous speaker] said, material things, and then boys care more about like sports and skills and music, like instruments, I think boys get more competitive over that side.
>
> (Joe, City High, Group One, Session One)

Although such skills are not particularly muscular displays in the ways that sport may be, physicality is nevertheless a big part of what Joe sees as being important to boys. This suggests that the properties of hegemonic masculinity continue to play a significant role in how young people conceive of boys' tastes and what is considered to be appropriate for them.[3]

Furthermore, boys are able to display appropriate taste by distancing themselves from the forms of music that are associated with girls. For example, typically feminine genres of music, such as pop tend to foreground singing rather than instrument playing, allowing for a distinction between 'feminine music' and 'masculine music' to be made. By focusing on technical ability a more 'serious' version of music and its appreciation becomes associated with boys, whereas in relation to girls the feminine value of music is considered to be much more trivial.

Masculinity and Appropriate Tastes for Boys

I make the case for why it is that girls are associated with pop music in the following chapter, but it is useful here to reflect on *how* boys distance themselves from 'girly' music in their (re)production of masculinity during boyhood.

> Interviewer: Would boys not go for One Direction?
> Mary: Yeah coz they're jealous!
> Juan: No.
> Josh: No definitely not.
> Phoebe: No! Shush! My little brother does and he's six.
> Juan: Unless you're [male name redacted].
> Josh: [laughing] Yeah!
> (City High, Group Two, Session One)

In this quote we clearly see distanciation from the pop group One Direction by the boys in the group. We also see in the above conversation some of the ways in which young people learn that One Direction are not appropriate to like. Phoebe remarks that the only boy she knows who likes One Direction is her six-year-old brother, thus rendering the taste childish for boys. Juan comments about a boy they know that would like the pop act, and this individual is publicly ridiculed and laughed at, regulating performances of masculinity in the process. In one case, Sara at City High comments that a boy that listened to pop artist Jessie J would probably be labelled 'camp', something boys are fearful of in the hyper-regulatory space of High School. This fear of homosexualisation experienced by boys during youth can also be evidenced in the performance of (hetero)sexual desire in articulations of taste. It is here then that we can understand vocal heavy rap as not problematic for boys, as it is associated with 'authentic' 'urban' masculinities and in particular 'tough' people of colour (see Frosh, Phoenix and Pattman 2002: 150–1).

Boys Like: Sexy Girls

> 'Because she has like, rather big boobies, so boys like her.'
> (Joe, City High, Group One, Session Two)

Discussion of 'glamour' celebrities such as British model and television personality Jordan/Katie Price and American model and actress Megan

Girls Like This, Boys Like That

Fox[4] allow us to see how liking some celebrities allows boys to articulate appropriate tastes. In the case of celebrity – which I demonstrate in the following chapter to be a topic of conversation overwhelmingly associated with girls – glamour models allow boys to perform heterosexuality by aligning themselves with these women through the male gaze. For example, Melark commented, 'if they were like the popular type of guy they would probably have, models and actresses in celebrities I like just to show off to their friends' (Girls High, Session Two). Such celebrities are therefore appropriate for boys to like because there is an assumption that boys only view them from the position of the male gaze. Numerous comments across the focus groups alluded to Price's physical appearance as central to why they though that a preference for her would belong to a boy. However, in terms of Katie Price, in many instances it was girls (re)producing this discourse rather than boys, with girls making the following comments; 'boys would probably go for her because [...] she's got nice curves' (Owls, Girls High, Session Two); 'they're [boys] not in it for her personality' (Phoebe, City High, Group Two, Session Two); 'they like looking at her!' (Mary, City High, Group Two, Session Two). This is in contrast to Troy at Outskirts High who commented that 'she used to be *alright*, she wasn't like the best, but she does just look proper plastic like uncanny valley too clean'[5] (Outskirts High, Session Three). As I will demonstrate in the following chapter, girls' critique of celebrity is central to the perception of their taste cultures, while boys are expected to be much less 'fussy'.

Such comments are similar to the ones made about Megan Fox. For example, 'she's what the boys look at on their phones, not a girl thing' (Eliza, Outskirts High, Session Three), and Joe demonstrated this in his active articulation of a preference for Megan Fox in the focus groups that he was a part of.

Interviewer: Let's go back to Megan Fox for a minute because –
Joe: – yeah, let's!
Interviewer: – it seems you didn't have a set opinion. What is it that you like so much about Megan Fox?
Joe: [laughs]
Leticia: Yeah, what do you like so much about Megan Fox, Joe?
Joe: I think she's rather beautiful.
[...]

Masculinity and Appropriate Tastes for Boys

Joe: [gestures 'breasts' by cupping his hands by his chest] Because she has like, rather big boobies, so boys like her, and girls sort of like, I think girls, they don't like her coz, either they think she's fake, and don't like her how [.] she's, like, yeah I don't think that they like that every boy likes her, in a way.
Erica: I don't think that's true.
Pedro: I'm partial to her.
Erica: I just don't have any interest in Megan Fox because she's just not into the films that I really like, so.
Joe: Exactly, I don't think any girl would have an interest in Megan Fox because, for any reason.
Interviewer: You're shaking your head at the back there.
Mel: I just don't think that girls really like Megan Fox, like, I don't know.
Joe: Because boys go on about her too much.
Erica: You [Joe] do talk about her.
Joe: Sorry!

(City High, Group One, Session Two)

A range of gendered assumptions are being made in this snippet of conversation. In terms of masculinity (I will consider the assumptions made about girls' judgements in the following chapter) we can see that Joe is able to perform heterosexual desire toward Fox and thus align himself with heterosexuality. Joe also dismisses that girls could like Megan Fox because he assumes that she is liked solely because of her attractiveness. In the other group at City High, Phoebe did suggest that girls could like Megan Fox, but there was an assumption that any girl who did like Megan Fox would be a 'lesbian' – this comment was followed by laughter which also suggests that this would be an unlikely and incongruous situation. This shows that girls *could* like something that has value in terms of masculinity, but only if the individual inhabited a masculine position and adopted the (heterosexual) male gaze.

What the examples of Katie Price and Megan Fox demonstrate is that (hetero)sexual desire is (re)produced in young people's sense-making of what is valuable in terms of masculinity. We see that Fox and Price are positioned as sexual objects, and so by saying they like such celebrities boys are able to align themselves with heterosexuality. This follows the work of Mac an Ghaill who has argued that 'the functions of young men's sex talk was publicly to validate their masculinity to their male friends' (1994: 92). This is important because as the following conversation shows, boys remain fearful of being homosexualised:

> Pedro: Coz if it was a boy they'd want to be [.] they don't want to [.] portray themselves as feminine.
> Flora: It's alright for a girl to be tom boyish but not so much for a boy to be like a girl.
> [Erica nods]
> Erica: If a boy says anything a bit like a girl they'll call them gay.
> Flora: ... **gay.**
> Leticia: That's because society, no.
> (City High, Group One, Session Four)

By saying they like celebrities such as Fox and Price, boys minimise the opportunity for others to label them gay. This is significant in the hyper-regulatory space of high school.

Concluding Remarks

Throughout the discussions held with young people, the perseverance of hegemonic masculinity is clear. Young people read gender into cultural texts and, in particular, skill and physicality were emphasised as being appropriate for boys to like. Boys like things such as sport, and action films, and rock music and looking at attractive women; boys don't want to be labelled gay. Within those texts deemed appropriate for boys to like, the case can be made that the masculine value lay in their representation (symbolic or literal) of the proponents of hegemonic masculinity.

The ways in which physicality was discursively (re)produced as having masculine value (and thus appropriate for boys to like) is significant in light of the concerns of youth masculinity as connected to physical violence and aggression (Frosh, Phoenix and Pattman 2002: 1; Gilbert and Gilbert 1998: 13), the 'crisis of masculinity' (Abbott 2013; Nayak and Kehily 2008: 43), and the negative impact that the failed promises of hegemonic masculinity have been theorised as having on the lives of boys (Consalvo 2003). All of the otherwise mundane activities of discussing the things that they like can therefore be seen as contributing to a wider, toxic masculine culture.

Masculinity and Appropriate Tastes for Boys

Given that gender operates on a spectrum it will therefore be useful to explore the role that femininity plays within youth taste cultures. As already alluded to, boys distance themselves from feminine texts for fear of being homosexualised, so what I will show in the chapter that follows are the texts that are considered to have feminine value. Furthermore I will show that boys' distanciation from feminine texts leads to many girls distancing themselves from them too. Masculinity may be in crisis, but it is also toxic, and for people of all genders. As I will show in the next chapter, the value placed on masculinity has a considerable impact on how girls engage with cultural texts and how they talk about what they like.

5

Girls Like That: Femininity and Appropriate Tastes for Girls

'It's a girl thing.'

(Phoebe, City High, Group Two, Session Two)

From Malala Yousafzai to Tavi Gevinson, riot grrrls to Spice Girls, girls are being celebrated like never before, and yet what I show in this research is that the subject position of 'girl' is one that is taken up with caution. Following in the footsteps of Jessalynn Keller I find the word 'girl' to be a powerful one, 'girl as an affect with political potential' (2016: 4). But, as with Keller and the girl participants of her study into the feminist blogosphere, I show that young people have a complex relationship with the label, with some embracing it and others rejecting it. What is it about 'girl' that offers dissatisfying possibilities? More specifically in terms of this book, what role does taste play in the (re)production of these discourses?

Girls find themselves at a double disadvantage; they are disadvantaged because they are young, and they are also disadvantaged because they are female. When it comes to the lives of girls in the West, anxieties have been articulated in both academic and popular discourse. In the case of British girls more specifically, girls don't seem to be able to win; they are all at once too sexual, too successful, too aggressive (see Ringrose 2013). While many girls seem to feel they are too fat, everyone else seems to be worried that they are too thin. And although there is much concern reserved for the lives of girls, they find themselves in the unlikely bind of being a site of celebration as well as of anxiety.

As Jessica Ringrose has written 'girlhood is constantly articulated through competing modes of celebration *versus* crisis' (2013: 4, emphasis in original). Girls are celebrated for their can-do attitudes (Harris 2004a), and their youthful femininities are understood as flexible, responsive and adaptable to the neoliberal imperatives of our time (Harris, 2004a; McRobbie 2009). And, of course, all of these gains for girls have been described (in popular debate at least) as the cause of boys' shortcomings, boys' failures and the crisis of masculinity (see Faludi 1999; Ringrose 2013: 2; Chapter 4 this volume).

No one knows these conflicting narratives better than girls themselves. Alongside the collection of the data that this book draws upon I have also been running a girl empowerment group, Day of the Girl, Norwich, since the UN Launch of International Day of the Girl Child in 2012. In our annual community exhibition that shows work created by girls and responds to the theme of 'what does it mean to be a girl?' we consistently receive artworks that grapple with the sophisticated discourses surrounding contemporary British girlhoods. Alongside these works, and in the conversations that I have with young people and fellow youth workers, a picture of the challenges that girls face is clearly painted. These girls from Norfolk have been articulate and critical of systems of oppression, but nevertheless acknowledge the impact that these discourses have on their lives. The girls I have engaged with discuss body image concerns, bullying and double standards (compared to boys). These girls also describe the pleasures they gain from being female, their strong friendships, creativity in their clothes and appearance, and strong female role models across time and space.

Of much of the work that has explored contemporary girlhoods, few offer an account without acknowledging the influence of postfeminism on Western girls' experiences. The 'postfeminist sensibility' (to use Gill's (2007) term) is one where feminism has had its day, repudiated either because it is seen to be an unachievable goal, or more often because the goals of feminism are assumed to have been achieved and that feminism is simply an unnecessary politic. It has also been argued that the emphases that neoliberal postfeminist rhetoric places on self-making and individualism have had a profound impact on how girls are seen as being able to enjoy new freedoms and opportunities (Harris 2004b: 8) and has thus impacted girls' engagement with femininity on a broad day-to-day level (Gill and Scharff 2011; Keller 2016; McRobbie 2009). However, while discourses of postfeminism have impacted the theoretical landscape with regard to how femininities and girlhood have been conceptualised, there remain relatively few empirical studies that explore how femininities are negotiated within the context of taste articulation.

In this chapter I show that girls have a complex relationship with what may not be considered 'appropriate' for them as girls, and explore the complexities of femininity in young people's lives compared to the *relative* straightforwardness of masculinity. This complexity is due to the devaluation of the feminine in a patriarchal context and the resulting ways in which girls do not align themselves with femininity in the same ways that I found boys do with masculinity. Indeed in a number of cases I found that girls also aligned themselves with masculinity, further complicating our understanding of the (re)production of gender within contemporary youth taste cultures. To work through these complexities I examine the (few) instances where texts were inscribed with value, and think about the grounds on which these values are allocated. I then turn to cases where *ways* of articulating tastes are gendered as feminine by participants. In doing so the (re)production of gender within contemporary youth taste cultures is elucidated. Before discussing these empirical findings I outline the developments that have been made within the burgeoning field of girlhood studies.

Theorising Girlhood and Femininity: The Background

Given the conversations that I have had with fellow academics at conferences as well as in everyday conversations I would first like to outline why I have chosen to use the word 'girl'. Women are routinely infantilised within everyday and media culture by being termed 'girls' and thus it is perhaps not surprising that the word has attracted criticism. However, I want to mobilise the political potential of the word 'girl', and thus I use it throughout this book and in my research more broadly. Of the other words that I could use I am keen to distance the female participants from the biology inferred in the world 'female' as well as the ways in which 'young woman' places girls at a particular stage on the path to (inevitable) womanhood; after all, not all who spend their childhood as girls will lead their adult lives as women. I also find the word 'child' somewhat problematic as it is not only genderless (for the most part), but it is also not a word that has been found to have resonance with young people themselves (see Thorne 1993). I instead seek to highlight the constructedness of both youth and gender through the use of the term 'girl' in this book. I understand 'girl' as referring to a particular way of being young and gendered as female (and thus discursively connected with femininity). Importantly I see girl as not being an *essentially* female category. Nevertheless I acknowledge that, as with femininity, the concept 'girl' is 'slippery' and not unproblematic (Harris 2004b: xx), but I feel that this slipperiness is part of its strength, and captures at least some of the nuances of youth and gender. Furthermore, as Keller (2016: 3) has highlighted, there are a variety of identities that intersect with girlhood such as race, class, and (dis)ability (to name a few) and thus it would be remiss to imagine that there is a singular understanding of girlhood available (see Pomerantz 2009), further suggesting the need for a somewhat slippery (or at least malleable) concept.

Femininities

A surprisingly large number of studies and theories that are concerned with the nature of femininity pay little or no attention to what 'femininity' is, as a concept, theory or 'lived category' (see Paechter 2012 for a discussion of this). Meanwhile Gill and Scharff have written of how there has been a wealth of exploration into 'hegemonic masculinity' (as demonstrated in the previous chapter), with little, if anything, written on 'hegemonic femininity' (2011: 12). If we conceive of hegemony as concerned with power and the reproduction of domination accepted within the status quo (see Gramsci 1979), then it is perhaps likely that femininity simply does not hold power in the way that masculinity does.

In the past, understanding femininity has, broadly speaking, 'address[ed] the qualities of being female, which are varied, multiple and time-place contingent, but are normalised along a social spectrum of social acceptability of what it is 'to be a woman'' (Thomas 2008: 64). Ideas

Femininity and Appropriate Tastes for Girls

of what it means 'to be female' are discursively (re)produced, and I show in this chapter the ways in which these discourses are deployed by young people to make sense of their friends' and peers' tastes. The subordinate position that femininity occupies in relation to masculinity (regardless of the internal hierarchies within these categories) makes femininity a less than desirable subject position to occupy. Seeing how girls (in particular) negotiate femininities is therefore a particularly fascinating site of study, and has been the subject of considerable academic debate within the burgeoning field of girlhood studies, not just over the decades (Griffin 1985; Hey 1997; McRobbie 1991; Walkerdine 1997) but particularly in recent years (Currie, Kelly and Pomerantz 2009; Driscoll 2002; Hains 2012; Harris 2004b; Keller 2016; Orenstein 2012; Ringrose 2013). While illuminating and rich bodies of work, these explorations of girlhood rarely (if at all) consider the role that masculinity and boys play in girls' negotiations of gender (in any great depth), an area that this book seeks to redress.

We, as social actors, are all complicit in the (re)production of femininity as having lower gendered value than masculinity. This is because not only has patriarchy systematically devalued it, but the concept of femininity has been at the centre of intense feminist scrutiny from the early stages of the second wave to this day. Furthermore, from the position of feminist politics, rather than working within the parameters of femininity, some feminists have sought to dispose of the category all together (Gauntlett 2008: 11). When this is considered in relation to the suspicions of earlier feminists and the 'trappings' of femininity (Baumgardner and Richards 2004: 61) and is routinely seen as 'more of a stereotype of a woman's role from the past' (Gauntlett 2008: 11), we can better understand how and why femininity operates in a very different context to masculinity, and thus why it remains fruitful to investigate femininity separately.

By thinking about femininity as distinct from masculinity (as well as femaleness) we can gain a sense of what femininity *means* for young people. Femininities have often been the site of academic interrogation when it comes to the lives of girls (for an overview see Aapola, Gonick and Harris 2005) and this book will contribute in part to these conversations. But I will also show how and why it is necessary to think of femininity as distinct from 'girlness', not least because this is a practice that the participants in this study routinely engaged in.

The Complexities of Femininity in Lived Realities

I show in this chapter that in many instances girls actually distance themselves from femininity when they talk about their own preferences, but also (re)produce a clear picture of the 'typical' feminine girl. I also show that girls take opportunities to playfully embrace the pleasures that femininity allows for them. With this in mind, I work through the highly nuanced experiences that girls (in particular) were found to negotiate, in a context where competing patriarchal, feminist and postfeminist discourses have informed what femininity can and/or should be. Following Anoop Nayak and Mary Jane Kehily I argue that cultural consumption (and in this case taste cultures) offer 'opportunities where femininities can be endlessly produced, defined and enhanced' (2008: 141). But unlike Nayak and Kehily, I believe that the genders here do not 'operate simultaneously as imagined and ideal everyday practice' (2008: 142). This is because the femininities that the participants discussed in this study did not appear to confer much value. The lingering presence of 'traditional femininity' meant that the girls' femininities were unable to confer cultural power, often leading the participants to reject it.

Within the findings that I present in this chapter, discourses of 'what girls do' were central to how young people understood *other people's* feminine cultural consumption. However, when it came to their own tastes the participants who presented as female were keen to demonstrate their agency and opposition to these dominant discourses of feminine taste. In many cases the dominant discourses of femininity were (re)produced as a marker against which many girls did *not* want to be seen (and of course boys too). These 'stubbornly persistent' (to use Gill and Scharff's (2011: 2) terminology) 'traditional' femininities were seen as offering dissatisfying possibilities in terms of what the girls felt they could *do* with them. The dissatisfying possibilities offered by these discursively dominant understandings of femininity can help us to see why femininity is understood by young people as holding lesser value than masculinity (for the most part). In the (re)production of this understanding, we can better make sense of how discourses of femininity as without value remain discursively dominant. And, of course, there are moments where this is complicated in lived contexts. For example, feminine 'skills' such as caring and listening were understood by participants to be highly valuable and meaningful.

Femininity and Appropriate Tastes for Girls

It seems therefore, that the role of femininity in young people's taste cultures is anything but straightforward.

Before I discuss the texts that were inscribed with feminine value, I first present the key findings from the identity pages and consider the complexities of girls' tastes in relation to these findings. We can therefore begin to think about the value of femininity in relation to the variety that was found in the identity pages.

Girls' Tastes, Femininity and the Identity Pages

The identity pages showed that girls tended to offer a wider range of responses than those given by boys. While some cultural texts, such as romance texts, were more present in the responses of those who described themselves using female descriptors, there were fewer texts or themes that recurred on girls' identity pages than there were for boys (such as football-related texts, as discussed in the previous chapter). This indicated that while there was nuance and diversity in the responses across genders, this was particularly pronounced in the responses given by girls. As I suggested in the previous chapter, this diversity problematises attempts to draw conclusions on the grounds of gender. However, when given to the participants in the focus groups, a clear understanding of how these tastes could be understood was demonstrated. This allows us to see how femininity is (re)produced when young people discuss the tastes that they imagine (or experience) as belonging to girls.

In many cases girls' taste cultures were considered as lesser in terms of femininity than boys tastes were in terms of masculinity. This is to say that boys appeared to be much more tied to masculinity than girls were to femininity. Instead, participants tended to see girls' tastes as residual ones, whereby if it was not 'definitely a boy' (displaying texts solely congruent with masculinity), then the assumption would be that the tastes belonged to a girl. Such assumptions follow the broader identity pages (on the whole) as they further demonstrate the variety and the wider potential of girls' tastes. That said, this may suggest that 'anything goes' as far as girls' tastes are concerned and the focus groups revealed that it was much more complex than this. I show that although girls can make taste articulations that favour texts with masculine value, the feminine is not necessarily rejected. Furthermore, on some occasions when girls' preferences with masculine value were discussed, I found that these too could be problematised, and this is something that I explicate in relation to participants, Leticia (City High, Group One), Naomi (City High, Group Two), Anna (Outskirts High) and Melark (Girls High) in the following chapter. Such participants and their tastes highlight the importance of actually speaking to young people and undertaking empirical research, as it is only through this approach that we can begin to work through the complexities of what young people's taste cultures *mean* and how they are experienced.

Following the structure taken in the previous chapter, I first explore the idea of feminine value and how it operates within contemporary youth taste cultures. This is before I examine the ways in which femininity is read into ways of *articulating*. This provides a solid understanding of how femininity operates in relation to youth taste cultures, and can help to contextualise the distanciation from femininity that I examine in the final chapter of this book.

Feminine Value

The pervasiveness of hegemonic masculinity within contemporary culture meant that it was relatively straightforward for the participants to discuss texts holding masculine value, as well as for me to identify them in this research (see for example Joe's discussion of 'conflict, action, violence' in the previous chapter). The identification of texts with feminine value is much more complex, and this is largely due to the lack of consensus as to what femininity means and what value it holds (or can hold) within a patriarchal context. Developing an understanding of why it is that femininity is discursively (re)produced as having less cultural value than masculinity is therefore useful not only in terms of understanding youth taste cultures, but also for the wider feminist field that is concerned with the reproduction of masculine value(s).

Early feminist media studies audience research has found that for some (female) audiences great pleasure can be gained from the consumption of feminine texts and that much of this pleasure is located within its very feminineness (Ang 1985; Modleski 1984; Radway 1987). With this in mind it would not be surprising to find that some young people like texts that hold feminine value. But of course, liking something is different to articulating a preference for something, which is when taste becomes public. While the aforementioned studies found that there is pleasure to be found in the consumption of feminine texts, they tell us little of how these pleasures are negotiated in relation to dominant discourses of gender and value by young people in the contemporary cultural context.

While I have argued that boys may articulate a preference for something with masculine value as a means of 'buying immunity from stigma' (to use McCormack's (2012) terminology), it is difficult to imagine how this would be the case for girls with respect to femininity. This is because in the patriarchal context it is hard to see how the feminine is able to confer power. However, femininity not being able to confer value or status onto the person articulating a preference for it does not mean that the text itself cannot be inscribed with value in terms of femininity anyway. If a text can be inscribed with masculine value and be considered important in terms of masculinity, then we can conceive of a similar process taking place with femininity. In the case of masculinity I found that texts were inscribed with masculine value if they represented or conveyed the proponents of hegemonic masculinity in some way. Existing research has argued that there can be no hegemonic femininity (Connell 1987; Gill and Scharff 2011; Paechter 2006) because '[f]emininities are not constructed in the same ways masculinities are; they do not confer cultural power, nor are they able to guarantee patriarchy' (Paechter 2006: 256). Instead, terms like 'emphasised femininity' (Connell 1987) or 'hyperfemininity' (Paechter 2006) have been used to describe the dominant idea(l)s of what femininity is. In this book I understand the femininities that are inscribed into texts as being 'traditional (emphasised/hyper) femininities'. This is because their values mirror the past femininities which people like Gauntlett (2008) have described as being how femininity is often understood. When participants talked about the texts that they understood as valuable in terms of femininity these sorts of 'traditional' properties were common features. For example, romance texts were the main area seen to be valuable in terms of femininity (also discussed in the aforementioned 1980s feminist media studies works of Ang, Modleski and Radway). In romance texts affective elements such as emotionality were seen by participants to be of particular significance to female audiences. It is perhaps interesting to note that while participants had a clear sense of what had masculine value, they were much less clear about what had feminine value. Instead, there were *ways* of articulating taste that participants understood as being gendered, with particular reasons for liking texts such as (hetero)sexual longing or an interest in the private that were understood as feminine. I also found that some of the boys in the group described how the emotionality of femininity was something that they too considered to be valuable, demonstrating that boys can and sometimes *do* see value in the feminine. As such it would be inaccurate to describe the role of femininity in contemporary youth taste cultures as anything but complex.

Broadly speaking, understanding feminine value allows us to think about how girls are able to 'enjoy' a greater breadth of appropriate tastes because cultures of the feminine are found to have been symbolically *de*valued (by both boys and girls). This is a double-edged sword because girls are only awarded freedoms in their tastes because 'being girls' means that they are already associated with femininity (which has diminished value). Furthermore, I would add that this rejection of the feminine is a privilege awarded to cis-girls, as trans-girls are likely to have a much more complex relationship to femininity in their performance of gender as well as their sense of belonging to feminine culture. Equally, this devaluation of the feminine limits the articulations that boys are able to make (cis and trans). Boys' preferences for texts with feminine value were often problematised, (re)producing masculinity in the process. In order to better understand these complexities I work through the few areas inscribed with feminine value, romance texts, before discussing how girls' tastes were understood through other means such as mode and motivation of articulation.

Girls Like: Romance

Feminine value was inscribed by participants into romance texts on the grounds that they contain and represent elements of love and intimate relationships, which participants saw as being of interest to girls. The inscription of feminine value into romance texts was observed across a range of cultural forms, with participants locating the 'femininity of romance' within songs, movies and television programmes to name a few. In *many* cases participants connoted romance with femininity so heavily, it was so 'obvious', they did not even feel they needed to explicitly say it was for girls. For example, when speaking hypothetically Josh said that if

Femininity and Appropriate Tastes for Girls

someone said they liked a romance text it *'could have definitely given it away* [as being a girl]' (City High, Group Two, Session One). Assumptions made about girls' tastes show the ways in which romance texts are understood to be feminine. This is not to say that participants uncritically accept that girls (essentially) like romance, but rather that through the association between femininity and girls' tastes this discourse is dominant.[1]

A range of discursive devices were used by participants that (re)produce notions of romance as being 'inherently' feminine. One of the main strategies was to connect feminine 'skills' such as maintaining relationships and having an interest in love and emotion with girls (and women more broadly). As such, the association between girls and romance was pervasive and demonstrated in conversations across the focus groups. For example, when discussing the television programme *90210* (The CW 2008–2013) participants at City High discussed its focus on relationships as having feminine value for girls.

Phoebe: It's a girl thing.
Mary: Yeah it's –
Naomi: – it's about relationships.
Phoebe: You don't really get many boys on there.
Juan: Because it's seen as a girl's thing many boys wouldn't even give it a try.
Mary: It's a lot about relationships and boys don't really give a damn about relationships.
Rachel: Yeah.
(City High, Group Two, Session Two)

This excerpt also illustrates the relationality of gender, with 'what boys do' figuring in why participants think girls like television programmes such as *90210*. We also see in this quote that the show's emphasis on love and relationships is what makes it of interest to girls (and relationally not boys). It is also noteworthy that Phoebe identifies the lack of boys on the programme as offering a further reason for boys not seeing value in it.[2] Given that masculine value was found in sport (predominantly men's football), we can also think about the role that the visibility of different genders plays in the inscription of gendered-appropriateness. The findings thus far suggest that a text foregrounding lots of boys/men is going to be read as appropriate for boys, whilst the foregrounding of women/girls will be read as appropriate for girls. Given the fragility of masculinity and the fluidity of femininity, it may follow that the foregrounding of trans, queer and non-binary folk would also be read as inappropriate for boys under patriarchy.

When it came to the conversations about film, discourses of romance having feminine value, and thus being appropriate for girls to like, were found across the focus groups. Romance was mentioned specifically on just one of the prompts and yet featured predominantly in participants' discussions of gendered taste. The feminine value of romance was clearly demonstrated at City High, when Phoebe made reference to a 'typical girl', leading me to ask her what she understood a typical girl to be:

> Phoebe: A typical girl, like how they've been put out, is to watch –
> Sara: – like Glee –
> Phoebe: – yeah romance and stuff.
> Sara: Chick flicks.
> Mary: Yeah, I'll watch romcoms or whatever, I'll happily –
> Lauren: – yeah I know loads that watch romcoms.
> (City High, Group Two, Session One)

Interestingly, with the exception of Mary (and later Rachel), all of the girls in this conversation distanced themselves from this idea of the 'typical girl'. For example, rather than saying 'girls watch', Phoebe problematises the idea, describing the 'typical girl' in a way that highlights its artifice, saying 'how they've been put out is …'. Similarly, when Lauren says, 'I know loads' she too dis-aligns herself with the position of 'typical girl'. In Group One at City High, Portia also used this way of talking about girls, saying 'I think a lot of girls like chick flick sort of films' (Session One). In doing so Portia (re)produces the idea that girls like chick flicks, but dis-aligns herself from the subject position by avoiding saying 'I like chick flicks'. She furthermore states that she 'thinks' rather than 'knows', indicating that she is not necessarily an expert on feminine tastes. This is vastly different to how boys claim knowledge over masculinity, where discussions of Chuck Norris allowed boys to 'mansplain' the star and the cultural currency that he holds to the girls in the group. This is an important distinction as it suggests that girls do not readily identify with feminine subject positions, an area to which I return later in this chapter in the discussion of girls and their 'guilty pleasures'.

Femininity and Appropriate Tastes for Girls

However, not all girls distanced themselves from romance texts, demonstrating the complexity of femininity in girls' taste cultures. For example, in a discussion about the tastes of a prompt-writer who said they did not like romance texts, Anna exclaimed '*he*[3] *dislikes romance films; they are like my thing, I will watch romance over anything*' (Outskirts High, Session Two). Positive articulations were also taken up by (some) girls at City High:

Primrose:	Most [girls] like romance films.
Melark:	It's just stereotypical ... I like Alien Versus Predator.
Primrose:	Yeah but every time you go to a sleepover or something you always watch romance films
Rue:	Yeah!
Primrose:	Coz it's like chick flicks.
Clove:	No actually we watched High School Musical. [laughter]
Rue:	That's a romance film!
Bea:	That's romance! [laughter]
Owls:	It's cheesy romance but its romance!

(Girls High, Session One)

Although Melark maintains distance from femininity by discussing romance as being 'stereotypically' for girls and cements this by asserting her own taste for a text high in masculine value, action film *Alien vs. Predator* (2004), the stereotypes that she highlights are nevertheless played out in the lived experiences of her peers. This shows us some of the ways in which although there is diversity in girls' experiences of feminine tastes, the discourses that are reproduced are part of a collective culture that is enjoyed by these girls (sleepovers). This follows the notion that romance is an integral part of girls' tastes. At Outskirts High, Eliza also saw preference for romance texts as being central to girls' tastes, exclaiming '*she doesn't like romance movies, what kind of girl is this?!*' (Session Three). For Eliza, not articulating a preference for romance leads to the questioning of this girl's assumed femininity. This makes the statement all the more interesting because it was one of the only instances in which a girl's taste was rendered questionable on the grounds that she did not like something that was inscribed with feminine value.

The final instance where the feminine value of romance was used to understand youth taste cultures was in providing an indicator for why girls might like something. For example, when considering British television programme *Misfits* (E4 2009–13), Troy discussed how it could be read as appropriate for either a boy or a girl to like. The logic behind his thinking lay in how the programme could be read in different ways, saying that 'it has all the romantic girly bits but then it's got the invisible guy [...] that will kill someone with a doorknob or something' (Outskirts High, Session Three). The discourses that underpin these assumptions are that romance has feminine value while violence holds masculine value (as discussed in the previous chapter). In a similar vein, I also showed in the previous chapter, in the discussion about death and the film *Titanic*, that it was the 'ultimate death' where the masculine value lay, while the romance was where the feminine value, and thus girls' interest, was located.

Through these inscriptions of gendered value, participants were able to label particular taste articulations as gender appropriate, even if the texts were the same (e.g. *Misfits*, *Titanic*) but the genders different. I have therefore revealed the assumption that young people have that liking romance would be gender appropriate for girls and therefore conforms to wider understandings of 'what girls like'. This is continued somewhat in the field of music, where the romantic content of songs was understood as feminine, as was the absence of instruments (which was shown in the previous chapter to have masculine value).

Girls Like: Singing and the Singers

> 'I think girls probably go for members more than boys do.'
> (Chloe, Outskirts High, Session One)

In the previous chapter I argued that music's masculine value was inscribed into cultural texts which displayed technical skill (following assumptions of the masculine as active/physical). The feminine value in music is therefore (relationally) *not* located within this area and instead understood in terms of superficial factors such as the gender and attractiveness of the acts/artists (e.g. young, male and 'conventionally' attractive). The second reason for music being inscribed with feminine value is if the song or back catalogue of the artist is lyrically focused around issues of love and romance

Femininity and Appropriate Tastes for Girls

(discussed above as being seen as central to girls' tastes). In the first instance, the attractiveness of the artist was central to understanding if it would be appropriate for girls to like, for example heterosexually normative male artists such as Justin Bieber and the members of One Direction or the Jonas Brothers were all cited as 'fit' and thus 'for girls'. However, this was a much more sanitised version of what I found with masculinity and boys' sexual objectification (discussed in the previous chapter). When discussing the band The Beatles, an act that Josh said he would listen to because *'they have good guitars and pianos'* (City High, Group Two, Session One), other groups discussed the band's (former) attractiveness (rather than their musicality) as offering an explanation for why girls may have liked them:

> I think when they were like big, in the sixties and stuff, probably, maybe women liked them because they were all like handsome and stuff, but now, it's [inaudible] I don't know, I don't think people probably fancy them anymore, coz they're all, o-old and dead and stuff.
> (Mel, City High, Group One, Session Two)

This illustrates the ways in which gender appropriate taste is (re)produced in the discussion of a cultural text that could be appropriate for either of the genders that I explore here to like. The feminine value for girls in The Beatles is clearly discussed by Mel as being (or as having been) located in the attractiveness of the members.[4] Artists and/or their songs could also be inscribed with gendered value if they are centred on romantic love, which is something common to pop music (Railton 2001). What also emphasises the feminine value of pop is that it foregrounds singing and not the playing of instruments (by the act/artist). Without the masculine value offered by the technical skill of instrument playing, singing can be considered feminine in its absence of explicitly masculine traits. This also follows and helps to explain Ashley's finding that 'boys regarded singing as sissy' (2011: 61). I also observed the feminine value of singing during the exploratory ethnography, where oftentimes I saw girls singing (during and between lessons), demonstrating Willett's (2011) finding that girls sing *much* more often than boys do during school hours.

When thinking about pop music more specifically, the feminine value of the genre was also discussed by participants in relation to how it has been marketed toward girl audiences. Phoebe suggested that 'it's more put out for girls' (City High, Group Two, Session One), adding that she thought that because the songs are largely about relationships they are not for boys. Therefore due to the absence of instruments coupled with the emphasis on singing (about romance), pop songs become an area of cultural life that is considered high in feminine value and thus seen as appropriate for girls, and not boys, to like.

All of these discourses surrounding feminine tastes and pop music serve to reproduce patriarchal values of the feminine as 'trivial'. I have written about some of the ways in which girls are able to politically subvert these discourses through gaining pleasure from the performance of fangirling elsewhere (see Cann 2015) and so here I want to focus on how the feminine becomes devalued within contemporary youth taste cultures.

With the oft-trivialised teenybopper forms of fandom associated with girls in the case of boygroups spanning The Beatles through to the Backstreet Boys (see Ehrenreich 2003; Wald 2002), and more recently One Direction (Dare-Edwards 2014; Korobkova 2014), each generation of the mass media age has had its own pop music fangirls. This is important because girls that engage and articulate preferences for pop music artists and acts are rarely conceived of as anything other than silly and inconsequential, a viewpoint rarely awarded to male fans. For example, when discussing girls' engagement with music (and this needn't only be pop) Sara notes that 'whereas boys listen to the music, girls just fangirl' (City High, Group Two, Session One). Sara therefore suggests that girls do not engage with the 'important' or substantive aspects of cultural texts. This idea is replicated at another site of study, where Anna describes how girls don't really engage with the stuff that 'matters', saying 'yeah coz she'd go all fangirl over them [mimicking] oh my god he looks so good!' (Outskirts High, Session One) In this instance the hypothetical girl Anna places emphasis on the *appearance* rather than the *substance* of the cultural text. Such responses to girls' perceived taste cultures allow us to see how cultures of femininity are seen to have low cultural value. The idea that boys *listen* to the music also further distinguishes girls' and boys' tastes, (re)producing discourses that render feminine subject positions trivial. This can have serious ramifications in the (re)production of gender and how people identify (or dis-identify) with them, demonstrating some of the more everyday ways in which the feminine is discursively devalued within contemporary youth taste cultures.

The performance of gender for girls and alignment with particular feminine taste subjectivities is therefore somewhat more complex than it is for boys with respect to masculinity. However, there were other ways in which girls were able to perform gender within taste cultures, and this was in the *mode* and *motivation* for articulating particular tastes.

Girls' Tastes and the (Re)Production of Gender Through Articulation: The Feminine Value of Bitching

> 'Girls get more bitchy about it.'
> (Eliza, Outskirts High, Session One)

Compared to the boys, there were far fewer texts inscribed with feminine value, and so discourses of femininity were (re)produced in girls' taste cultures in other ways. The main area was in *how* girls articulated their tastes, finding that there were particular forms of articulating judgement that young people understood as being unique to girls. By not only looking at what texts are liked or disliked, but also examining *how* taste is articulated we can develop a much richer understanding of the (re)production of gender in youth taste cultures. This provides an important interjection into the taste culture field as it emphasises the significance of *how* people talk about their tastes rather than simply *what* they say.

Generally speaking, girls were encouraged to 'say what they think' about others, leading to the wider culture of scrutiny and judgement theorised as prevalent within girl cultures (see Hey 1997; Kehily 2002; Renold 2005; Ringrose 2013). This led to a 'culture of bitching' that was associated with girls' taste cultures and is realised in a number of ways. In this section I will first outline how participants discussed bitching as being central to girls' lives, and then focus on instances where this can be seen in the articulation of taste relating to Katie Price.

Forms of critique within the articulation of taste can be understood as a form of bitching as it is a feminine form of talking that emphasises scrutiny and critique (Guendouzi 2001). Importantly, however, bitching is not innate to girls, and this bitching is something that boys could perform (at the risk of being shunned) too. In discussion of why it is they felt girls liked the social media platform Twitter more than boys, bitching was central to their understanding:

Sara:	Twitter's more of a girls' website –
Lauren:	–girls girl thing.
Rachel:	Yeah.
Interviewer:	Why do girls like Twitter more?
Phoebe:	Because you can rant about anything.
Rachel:	Yeah.
Naomi:	You can put some sweet quotes that are really disgusting.
Sara:	And you can follow One Direction and Justin Bieber in Naomi's case.
[...]	
Mary:	Don't you spend Twitter like bitching about people? I don't have Twitter so I don't know. [...]
Mary:	Naomi you have Twitter: do people, people bitch on Twitter like all the time?
Naomi:	Not always.
Sara and Lauren:	Yes.
Mary:	Yeah that's a girl.
	(City High, Group Two, Session Two)

Twitter is awarded feminine value due to its capacity to provide a space for bitching. This is best exemplified by Mary asking if people bitch on Twitter, and when Sara and Lauren confirm this, Mary uses the confirmation of the presence of the gendered value of bitching as a means of understanding a preference for Twitter as gender appropriate for girls.[5]

Whenever a relatively large number of celebrities were listed on a prompt participants discussed how they thought it was most likely a girl. This is again because they associated the feminine practice of bitching with the act of having an opinion on celebrity culture. Broadly speaking, the participants discussed celebrity culture, and more specifically having an opinion on particular celebrities, as something that girls 'do'. It is not that celebrities have inherently feminine value, but rather that in talking about expressing judgement/critique of particular celebrities, girls 'do'

Femininity and Appropriate Tastes for Girls

femininity. This is demonstrated in the following conversation about celebrity 'Marmite',[6] Justin Bieber.[7]

Katherine:	If it was a girl they would have probably put, celebrities I like Justin Bieber, or celebrities I dislike Justin Bieber.
Eliza:	It would be on one of them, he'd be on there.
Tom:	Mhm hm.
Anna:	When was this created?
Interviewer:	This time last year.
Anna:	Oh he was around so yeah.
Chloe:	Unfortunately.
Interviewer:	So all girls hate Justin Bieber?
Katherine:	Or love.
Eliza:	Unless you love him, he's Marmite.
Interviewer:	But everyone's got an opinion on him?
Anna:	Exactly…
Katherine:	Pretty much.
Anna:	… it's like Marmite you either love him or you hate him.
Chloe:	You can't escape him he's everywhere! You have to have an opinion.
Tom:	You have to burn him.

(Outskirts High, Session One)

Expressing an opinion (usually one of critique) allows girls to talk about the personal, a realm long associated with women and femininity (Sichtermann 1983). As demonstrated in the above conversation about 'Marmite' subject Justin Bieber, in most cases there was not a particular position on celebrity that was considered to be gender appropriate. Instead it was the act of 'having an opinion' that was deemed to be important for girls. In general, boys were described as not really caring about celebrities, but they could appropriately articulate preference toward a celebrity if they so wished (the identity pages revealed that boys did, and the discussions about Katie Price and Megan Fox detailed in the previous chapter showed how) and following this we see Tom above rejecting the appropriate-for-girls Bieber. The distinction is that girls were expected to be much more interested in the *lives* of celebrities, or at least express their feelings about a celebrity with more intensity than a boy would. Particular ways of articulating a preference (or dislike) for celebrities, as well as the reasons behind these judgements, were highly gendered. Female celebrities in particular were subject to considerable critique, often reflecting the anxieties that young people grapple with in their own experience of sexual regulation by peers in wider contemporary culture and the impossibility of achieving 'perfect femininity' (see Ringrose 2013: 90–1 for a useful discussion of this). The tensions and anxieties related to femininity experienced by girls can be seen in their discussions of the celebrities favoured by boys, and in particular Katie Price.

That female audiences do not often like Katie Price is not overly surprising given that it has been well documented in the academic literature (Skeggs and Wood 2008; Tyler and Benett 2010), but what is interesting here is that we can see how younger audiences negotiate this taste position, and how it can play a central role in the (re)production of gender. In many cases there were very broad claims made about 'girls' and their dislike of Katie Price. For example, at Outskirts High, Eliza simply said 'girls hate Katie Price' (Session Two). There is little nuance in how girls' tastes are understood here. There is no, 'most girls I know' nor 'a lot of girls' nor is there even an 'I don't like Katie Price', instead Eliza says 'all girls', demonstrating the centrality of this taste position within perceptions of girls' taste cultures. Eliza was not the only participant to speak in such terms, as for example at Girls High Primrose and Rue both said, 'girls *hate* her' (Session Two); meanwhile at City High Sara said 'girls don't like her' (Group Two, Session Four).

Generally participants focused on Price's appearance and claim to fame as a means of explaining why it is that girls do not like her, in many ways drawing on the dominant discourses of why Price has come to be read as a 'worthless' celebrity (Holmes 2005: 13).[8] The most common criticism that Price received was that she is 'fake' and that she 'thinks she's pretty but she isn't' – one of the major no-nos of femininity identified in Ringrose's (2013) work. This position is captured in the following exchange that took place at Girls High:

> Primrose: Girls hate her because she's fake she hasn't done anything to deserve celebrity.
> Bella: I think girls dislike her because they just think she's a fame seeker.

Femininity and Appropriate Tastes for Girls

Primrose: She is.
Bella: Like she's not that pretty.
Primrose: She's not.
Bella: And she's gone too far.
Primrose: She has.
Clove: I don't think she was pretty to start with!
[laughter]
(Girls High, Session One)

In this exchange an amusing pattern took place, with Primrose affirming Bella's statements about why it is that girls do not like Katie Price. In the opening stages of the conversation Bella is less certain about her theories, saying that she *thinks*. Meanwhile, Primrose *is* certain, cutting in to close down Bella's theories and to present them as immutable fact. The focus on Price's appearance as inauthentic and 'fake' emphasises the trend for 'effortlessness' in female presentation as a symptom of the postfeminist condition.

There were also some comments made that girls might be jealous of the attention and attractiveness of stars such as Price and Fox, and a couple of statements made about her sexualisation. For example, when discussing the distinction between Katie Price and her alter ego Jordan, Sara remarked, 'her slag side is Jordan isn't it? And like Katie Price is when she's not being a whore', to which Lauren responded 'which is never' (City High, Group Two, Session Four). In one other instance Tom at Outskirts High used the word 'slag' to describe how she looks (Session Three). Given that regulation on the grounds of sexuality has been found to play such a central role within contemporary Western girl cultures (Kehily 2004; Ringrose 2011, Ringrose 2013; Tolman 2009), that it was rarely mentioned in the focus groups in this research is notable. These findings show that disliking celebrities such as Katie Price is a gender appropriate taste position for girls, demonstrating that girls respond to glamour models much more critically than previous research may suggest (Coy and Garner 2010).

Concluding Remarks

This chapter has demonstrated the ways in which femininity is simultaneously understood and rendered of low cultural value within contemporary youth taste cultures. Unlike with masculinity, which was much more easily inscribed into cultural texts and aligned with by a variety of young people, feminine taste positions were seen to offer much less satisfying outcomes. Given the fear of being shunned and the pervasiveness of homophobia in contemporary British youth cultures it is only really girls who have the opportunity to identify with and perform feminine taste subjectivities. However, the prevalence of patriarchal values and the systemic devaluation of the feminine in contemporary youth taste cultures make this a somewhat uncomfortable subject position for girls to adopt. This is because, as Halberstam (1998) has argued, femininity is largely unable to confer power.

Regularly when girls did articulate preferences for things high in feminine value, such as a romantic film or a pop act like Justin Bieber, they would prefix their articulation by saying that it's 'a bit of a guilty pleasure'. A statement such as this allows a girl to make her feminine taste articulation whilst also not losing too much respect from her peers. This follows Paechter's claim that '[r]enouncing femininity thus becomes an act of renouncing powerlessness, of claiming power for oneself' (2006: 257), and allows us to understand how this works within contemporary youth taste cultures. Examples of texts which the girls mentioned as being a guilty pleasure are all ones that fit within the areas of romance, the personal and pop culture, including texts from across media such as *90210*, *Big Brother* (Channel 4 2000–2011; Channel 5 2011-present), One Direction, the book *50 Shades of Grey* (2011) and the *Twilight* film series (2008–2012). A further interrogation of how these tastes are worked out is the subject of previously published work (see Cann 2015).

Through terms such as 'guilty pleasure' and the distancation girls enacted from notions of 'girls' tastes', we can come to better understand how patriarchy works within contemporary youth taste cultures to devalue the feminine. What I will demonstrate in the following chapter are some of the nuances of gender in contemporary youth taste cultures. I will consider instances and spaces for transgression, as well as the reigning in of potentially subversive taste articulations.

6

Living on the Edge: Regulating and Transgressing Gender Appropriate Taste

'I think they'd get teased, I think it's quite sad but they would.'
(Erica, City High, Group One, Session Four)

Can a gender inappropriate articulation ever be accepted within the hyper-regulatory space of the high school? Transgressions, as well as potentially problematic taste articulations, can help us to better understand the complexities of the (re)production of gender in contemporary youth taste cultures. When I talk of gender transgression I should clarify that I am referring to moments of incongruity, when the gender attributed and the taste articulated do not 'match' and thus the stability of (cis)gender and its binary are troubled.

In the chapters that have preceded this one I have shown that young people have a clear sense of what sorts of cultural texts are 'gender' appropriate for them to like. While boys are expected to like the sorts of texts that fit with dominant discourses of hegemonic masculinity (like action films, sport, guitar-based music and sexy girls), girls were also expected to like 'girly' things like romance texts and pop songs (although there was considerably more fluidity awarded to girls in their lived realities than to boys). Notions of gender appropriate taste matter because, as I explored in Chapter 3, young people continue to place value in the gender binary. In almost all accounts given in the course of this research young people reinforced the existence of a gender binary, asserting that while one may 'act' differently under their performance lies a discoverable, and biologically fixed, gender identity. What this book has yet to fully explore then are the moments of transgression, where expected behaviour either is not performed, or where the certainty and knowability of gender is troubled.

In exploring moments of transgression, in this chapter I want to think about what 'queer' might mean for young people who sit relatively comfortably within the 'mainstream'. That is, young people who do not actively live 'queer lifestyles', such as those explored by the contributors of Susan Driver's edited collection *Queer Youth Cultures* (2008), but rather what could be considered otherwise 'normal'/'untroublesome' teen lives. In doing so I will draw on moments where boys have troubled hegemonic masculinity by aligning themselves with feminine texts, and explore what happens when girls 'over align' with feminine texts. I consider the extent to which these actions and articulations can even be deemed transgressive and the ways in which the group recuperates the acts within the heterosexual matrix. Furthermore, I discuss the complexities of gender appropriate taste, drawing on examples where boys 'over align' with masculine texts, bringing their own performances of gender into question. I therefore question the ways in which gender is collectively regulated for being either too masculine/feminine or not masculine/feminine enough.

Existing work in the field is still getting to grips with the application of queer theory to young people's lived realities, and there remain tensions (particularly in the field of young masculinity studies) with respect to the perceived openness to homosexuality experienced within contemporary youth cultures (see Steve Roberts' (2014) edited book on this topic, for example). Theorists such as Epstein and Johnson have found discrepancies in gender fluidity in youth, noting that while a girl aligning with masculinity can be interpreted positively, it does not work the other way around (1998: 168). Furthermore, Francis has argued that there is a 'powerful heterosexualisation of schools' (2010b: 32), which is heightened within the findings presented here of schools as hyper-regulatory. This suggests that performances of gender which trouble dominant discourses of appropriate taste are all the more risky during youth, and more specifically when performed at high school. As I show in this chapter, it is not simply enough to articulate the 'right' tastes but they also need to be, as Ringrose has argued, 'recognisable and intelligible within normative constraints' (2013: 71).

A significant factor in the transgression of gender is gender attribution, the process that Kessler and McKenna (1978) discuss as taking place when one decides if someone (else) is 'male' or 'female' – and given the discursive persistence of the gender binary as knowable and biologically rooted, this is likely still to be the process some 40 years later. In terms of gender transgression, McGuffey and Rich (1999) have argued for the existence of a 'gender transgression zone', a space where people transgress the boundaries of what is gender appropriate, and McGuffey and Rich's work has similarities to those posited in this book, that 'girls cross over more than boys and receive fewer sanctions for gender deviations' (1999: 617). But, as I explore in this chapter, these realities involve complex negotiation by the young people that live them.

To work through the nuances of gender transgression through taste articulation I first examine gender inappropriate taste articulations (and their consequences) for those who present as boys, an area that has been theorised as being considerably regulated (see Epstein and Johnson 1998; Mac an Ghaill 1994; Renold 2005). This is juxtaposed against transgressions for girls, where I raise the question of whether or not girls are able to meaningfully queer gender through taste articulation at all. I show that for boys there were much clearer and more problematic consequences for transgressing gender appropriate taste.

Gender Appropriate Tastes

In order to best understand how gender can be transgressed it is worth revisiting the findings of the previous two chapters to remind ourselves of the tastes that are deemed gender appropriate for boys and girls. Boys were found to be much more heavily constrained by discourses of hegemonic masculinity than could be said for the taste cultures of girls. For example, the 'norm' would be for boys to say they liked things such as watching *Match of the Day* or action films, whereas the 'norm' for girls would be to say they liked romantic films or pop stars like One Direction or Justin Bieber. By aligning themselves with such taste positions young people are able to perform discursively appropriate gender. However, in the previous chapter I showed that feminine taste positions were not always, in fact rarely, readily taken up by the girls that I spoke to; and this is in part due to the dissatisfying possibilities offered by the limited and limiting discourses of conventional femininity (Brown 1998). In this chapter I want to think about how young people carve out spaces for transgression; asking questions of how queer we can consider such actions to be. I will also show in this chapter how *over* alignment with particular gendered taste positions can also be rendered problematic by the group, drawing in particular on the example of the hyper-masculine tastes of a boy from the study. Within these discussions I demonstrate that taste and gender are highly nuanced during youth, requiring young people to be sophisticated and quick thinking in their performances of gender and articulations of taste.

Boys and Gender Inappropriate Taste

I have said much in Chapter 4 about the cultural power of masculinity and how participants had a clear sense of what sorts of cultural texts were appropriate for boys to like. Within these discussions I have demonstrated the centrality of hegemonic masculinity within these discourses, but what I have yet to comment on is what happens when these discourses are transgressed. What happens to boys who do not like sport? Are they shunned? If rejecting the masculine is about giving up power, as Carrie Paechter argues (2006: 256), what happens if boys actively align themselves with feminine taste subjectivities?

The sorts of things that are problematic for boys to like are the sorts of things that girls are expected *to* like (see previous chapter). This is because if boys say that they like 'feminine' things then their own gender expression becomes feminised through this alignment. This leads to their sexual identity being read as gay. This is only undesirable because 'gay' remains a problematic label for boys in the hyper-regulatory context of high school. Furthermore, in the focus groups I found that the boys who articulated a preference for feminine texts were often mocked, usually through homophobic means. Humour and other everyday forms of regulation (re)produced a somewhat narrow understanding of tastes deemed appropriate for boys. It is also useful to note at this stage that boys were also mocked for articulating 'too much' masculinity (as I will show below). Broadly speaking then, there is much evidence to suggest that in the younger age group of 14-year-olds, a much less inclusive masculinity than those evidenced by Anderson (2009) and McCormack (2012) was experienced. What I explore now is how boys are walking a tight-rope of gender appropriate taste.

To work through these nuances I draw on the responses made about two of the prompt-writers and their tastes. In one instance the boys' tastes were rendered problematic because they were 'too feminine', and in the other case it was rendered problematic because it was 'too masculine', demonstrating the fine line of gender appropriate taste that boys are forced to navigate and the potential ramifications of their transgressions.

Too Little Masculinity: Responses to Prompt Five

When I revealed to the participants that the person who wrote prompt five identified as male there was what could best be described as 'hubbub'. The participants made considerable fuss, looking shocked and gasping; they also spent time repeating aloud the texts that they felt were 'too feminine'

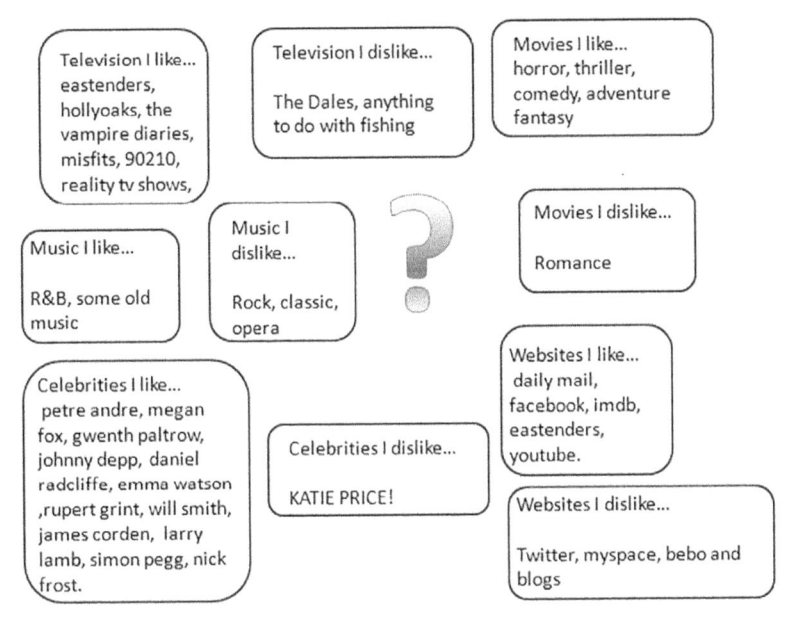

Television I like...
eastenders, hollyoaks, the vampire diaries, misfits, 90210, reality tv shows,

Television I dislike...
The Dales, anything to do with fishing

Movies I like...
horror, thriller, comedy, adventure fantasy

Music I like...
R&B, some old music

Music I dislike...
Rock, classic, opera

Movies I dislike...
Romance

Celebrities I like...
petre andre, megan fox, gwenth paltrow, johnny depp, daniel radcliffe, emma watson, rupert grint, will smith, james corden, larry lamb, simon pegg, nick frost.

Celebrities I dislike...
KATIE PRICE!

Websites I like...
daily mail, facebook, imdb, eastenders, youtube.

Websites I dislike...
Twitter, myspace, bebo and blogs

Figure 6.1 Prompt 5

for boys to say that they liked (such as *The Vampire Diaries* (The CW 2009–17), reality television programmes and Peter Andre). In Group Two at City High a few members of the group threw their heads back in shock or put their hands to their mouths while gasping. These embodied responses remind all present of the parameters of 'gender appropriate' taste. There were also verbal comments made that reinforced the boundaries of appropriate masculinity for boys. For example, after uttering some noises of disbelief a number of the participants repeatedly asked me 'really?!' and 'are you sure?!' assuming that I must have made an error. In response to this line of questioning, I asked the participants what might happen if one was to express these tastes at school:

> Interviewer: If this person said they liked all of these things at school...
> Erica: I think they'd get teased, I think it's quite sad but they would.
> [pause]
> Leticia: Yeah.
> Pedro: Nah, they'd fit in with the crew!
> Leticia: Oh ho ho ho ho.
> Reuben: In what crew?
> Erica: Leave them alone!
> Leticia: So awful!
>
> (City High, Group One, Session Four)

It is notable that Pedro (male) suggested that they could 'fit in with the crew' only for this to be ridiculed by his peers. Meanwhile, Outskirts High was the only place where explicit reference to the presumed non-heterosexuality of the boy was made:

> Interviewer: Number five was male 1995.
> Eliza: Ooh.
> Troy: Oh!
> Interviewer: Did anyone say male?
> Troy: No! ooh!
> Eliza: Oh!
> Interviewer: What?
> Anna: He likes The Vampire Diaries.
> [Tom flounces hand]

Chloe:	He likes Peter Andre.
Troy:	He seems a bit...
Interviewer:	Seems a bit what?
Anna:	[mouths the word 'camp' and then 'flounces' her hand]
Troy:	Flamboyant...
Tom:	Tom, Tom me.
Anna:	He's got gloves on.
Eliza:	He's got gloves on.
Anna:	He's got gloves on.
Eliza:	That's a family joke don't worry about it.

(Outskirts High, Session Three)

Similar responses were given at Girls High, where participants gasped and made comments such as 'no way' and 'really?!' repeatedly. Clove went so far as to say *'that's so wrong'* (Session Two). Interestingly they commented on the *combination* of texts as being particularly problematic.

Melark:	If it was just like one of the televisions I like you might be able to get away with it but all of them...
Primrose:	It's just so strange.

(Girls High, Session Two)

When participants discussed boys' transgressions of gender appropriate taste, in many cases the individual's sexual orientation was a central factor in how they imagined him. Participants discussed how gender inappropriate taste articulations could be made by somebody who was gay – and thus, in their eyes had abandoned the pursuit of masculinity in hegemonic terms. The significance of a feminine taste articulation made by a boy is usefully captured by a dramaturgical metaphor described by Erving Goffman: 'a single note off key can disrupt the tone of the entire performance' (1971: 60). Melark discusses this 'off note' above as being potentially salvageable, but a series of off notes could ruin a claim for masculinity within the hegemonic matrix. Notably, though, if boys were open about their preference for non-masculine texts then they could find themselves in a situation where they were not shunned by their peer group. For example:

Phoebe:	If they were known for being like that though, liking girls shows.

> Sara: If they were like camp or gay or something yeah from day one.
> Phoebe: Yeah.
>
> (City High, Group Two, Session One)

However, what we see here is the conflation of boys holding feminine tastes and a gay sexual identity. A boy who transgresses gender appropriate taste would be read as gay, regardless of whether or not he identified as such. This is significant because being labelled gay remains problematic, particularly in the homophobic hyper-regulatory space of high school (see Chapter 2). Being labelled gay is not something that boys can easily shake off should they want to.

At City High Phoebe discussed how if a gender inappropriate taste was expressed by a boy who wanted to maintain a hegemonic masculine identity he would find himself in difficult circumstances:

> Phoebe: It depends on the person and if people knew that they liked that sort of thing but if it was like a proper manly boy and then they said it then they would probably would get bullied.
>
> (City High, Group Two, Session One)

What I found to be a general consensus across the groups was that boys should avoid making any transgressive/feminine taste articulations should they want to present themselves as appropriately hegemonically masculine and thus 'not gay'. However, in the example I explore below, we will see that it is not as easy as simply aligning themselves with masculine taste subjectivities.

Too Much Masculinity: Responses to Prompt Three

> 'They're trying to assert their manliness.'
>
> (Erica, City High, Group One, Session Four)

The findings presented in this book thus far have largely conformed to what we already know about the operation of hegemonic masculinity during youth. In this section I demonstrate the limits of traditional forms of masculinity during youth, showing the ways in which aligning *too* heavily

Living on the Edge

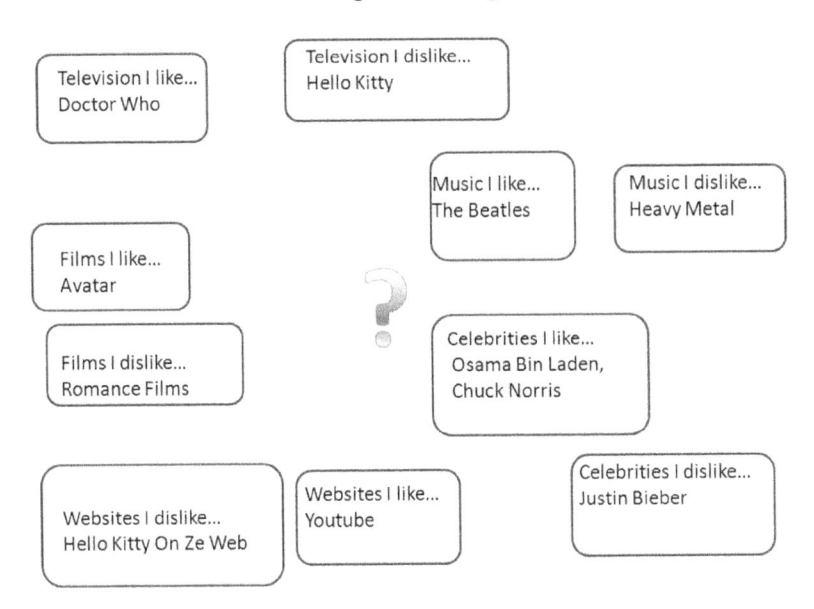

```
Television I like...          Television I dislike...
Doctor Who                    Hello Kitty

                              Music I like...      Music I dislike...
                              The Beatles          Heavy Metal

Films I like...
Avatar                    ?
                              Celebrities I like...
Films I dislike...            Osama Bin Laden,
Romance Films                 Chuck Norris

                                                   Celebrities I dislike...
                              Websites I like...   Justin Bieber
Websites I dislike...         Youtube
Hello Kitty On Ze Web
```

Figure 6.2 Prompt 3

with this subjectivity can also be rendered problematic. Discussions about boys who had tastes which were 'too masculine' emerged in response to the tastes of the person who in response to Prompt 3 described himself as a 'manly male'. In moments where we see this person's taste being mocked, where the prototypical hegemonic male is rejected by participants, the usefulness of Connell's theory of hegemonic masculinity is tested.

The discussions which took place across the focus groups revealed how a boy's expression of masculinity can be rendered inappropriate if he aligns with too many texts that have masculine value.[1]

The texts chosen by this prompt-writer can be seen to hold masculine value due to their proximity to conflict (including Osama Bin Laden and Chuck Norris) and his rejection of texts associated with feminine subjectivities (such as Justin Bieber and Hello Kitty). This combination of tastes led some group members to question the authenticity of his tastes, which were described as 'try hard' by many members. In the discussions that exemplify this (which took place during the 'Matching-Up Exercise') Reuben criticised the respondent for using the term 'manly male' to describe his gender. In this critique, Reuben lowered his voice so that it became very deep, mockingly saying *'manly male'* (City High, Group One, Session Four). By lowering his voice and pitch, Reuben draws on cultural understandings of hegemonically masculine men as having deep voices (see Jackson and Dangerfield 2002: 121). But rather than simply (re)producing the discourse Reuben mocks this form of masculinity, mirroring Cole's finding that older men do the same (2012: 5). Reuben therefore demonstrates the artifice of masculinity through performance. Within the focus groups participants mocked the prompt-writer for either being inauthentic, or for being someone 'trying to be funny' but ultimately failing to do so. At City High, one of the groups took issue with the prompt-writer for trying to be funny:

> Reuben: Well it's just –
> Erica: – just trying to seem so manly!
> Reuben: – they're trying to seem funny.
> Pedro: Yeah.
> Reuben: By saying manly male [.] In his eyes he's probably funny.
> (City High, Group One, Session Four)

The ridicule also took place in Group Two at City High, where Phoebe and Sara discussed how they believed this person *thought* that they were being funny, when in their opinion they were not. Sara suggests that the motivation for doing this would be as an attempt to be popular: *'like, trying to be funny to be popular'* (Sara, City High, Group Two, Session Two). That the participants rejected this humour follows from the idea that popularity and gender are two highly distinct parts of young people's lives, and thus one must not assume that to be *more masculine* is to therefore be *more popular*. This demonstrates some of the nuances of applying taste theory to the area of gender (it is not a simple field in Bourdeusian terms). It is nevertheless noteworthy that all of the participants did actually laugh when reading this prompt, suggesting that the prompt-writer was, at least in some part, successful in their aim, should it have been to elicit laughter.

At Outskirts High the response to this form of masculinity was to question the motivations of someone who would display it, whilst also using insults to describe the sort of person they thought it would be:

> Katherine: Vain.
> Chloe: Arrogant.

Troy:	Bit of a twunk.
Eliza:	Yeah, I'd say a vain person, describe your gender I'm a manly male, who says that?!
Chloe:	Clearly you're in denial about something!

(Outskirts High, Session Three)

In all of these cases, it was 'trying too hard' that was considered to be problematic, both in terms of a person's claim to masculinity and their presentation of identity more broadly. This follows Thornton's claim that '[n]othing depletes capital more than someone trying too hard' (1995: 12). Within the context of gender it seems that excessive articulations of preference for masculine texts can be readily rendered problematic and met with suspicion.

In the problematisation of excessive masculinity we see that the performance of hegemonic masculinity may not be as clear-cut as we might initially imagine. As I have shown above, 'not-being-feminine' is crucially important to boys, but we can see that so too is 'not-being-*too*-masculine'. This requires us to ask further questions of how we think about hegemonic masculinity during youth, as the performance of seemingly 'prototypical' hyper-masculine selves was not simply not-valued by participants in the group, but actively problematised.

Little Resistances?

However, we know that some boys *do* like cultural texts that are deemed 'feminine' and it is the strength of patriarchy that renders these taste subjectivities as out of reach for boys. Phoebe from City High commented that her brother would sneak to his room to read the copies of *Heat* magazine that they had in the house. I have also written elsewhere (Cann 2014) about how boys carve out 'safe spaces' for performances of masculinity that do not neatly fit within the hegemonic norm. In this work I discussed how some boys would seek refuge in tight-knit friendship groups where they knew that they could be more honest and open. But of course such tight friendships groups are not easy to come by, can be risky to develop, and require continued work from the boys within them. Humour can also provide spaces and contexts for little resistances, but through laughter, and ultimately such utterances are recuperated with the heterosexual matrix.

When taken at surface level, the acceptance of gender inappropriate taste articulations could be seen to support McCormack and Anderson's inclusive masculinity theory. However, when the bigger picture is taken into account, hegemonic masculinity is never really challenged because such articulations could only be accepted by the wider group if the boys who expressed them had already 'proved' their masculinity in other ways and at other times. This has important implications for how transgressive we can actually conceive of these taste articulations as being, as well as how inclusive we can say boys' cultures of masculinity actually are. The brief case studies of Joe (City High, Group One) and Tom (Outskirts High) provide an insight into some of the ways in which boys can perform seemingly transgressive taste subjectivities, whilst maintaining their status in the masculine hierarchy.

Joe

In one instance Joe enacted a feminine subjectivity whilst talking about the singer Lionel Ritchie. In this discussion Joe described the singer, saying 'I just think he's romantic and dreamy' (City High, Group One, Session Two). When the response from his classmate, Leticia was a warm '*ahhhh*' rather than laughter (which is what I think he expected), Joe quickly corrected himself by saying 'I don't actually like, I was just joking. I feel bad now'. In this moment of self-regulation Joe recuperates his masculinity. Notably though, Leticia did not laugh at him, nor did she make fun of him (none of his classmates did), and this is probably because they did not take his comment seriously. I make this claim because Joe had already anchored his identity as 'heterosexual' and thus his masculinity as appropriate within the hegemonic matrix through his previous articulations of taste and heterosexual displays with his girlfriend. Thus while some potentially problematic articulations were made by Joe, his masculinity was never really placed in threat, by virtue of his 'known' (performed) heterosexuality.

Tom

Tom also performed 'straight' on occasions while talking about his girlfriend but, unlike with Joe, Tom enacted much more fluid performances of gender. In the case of Tom humour played a central role in providing context for his moments of transgression and he would regularly draw on his position as 'class clown' (pulling faces, putting on funny voices and singing) whilst performing potentially transgressive tastes.[2] One of the recurring problematic articulations that Tom made was that he liked the television programme *Glee* (Fox 2009–15), which all focus group participants described as being 'for girls'. He would also routinely sing, something associated with girls within the context of school (Willett 2011), as well as make comments such as that above where he identified with the person that his peers said 'had gloves on'. While he did say that sometimes he was shunned, this seemed to be temporary and not damaging to his position in the masculine hierarchy at that school. However, despite all of this, Tom's (hegemonic) masculinity was never really in doubt. Tom's emphasis on humour meant that he was able to remind people that he was not really being serious, and furthermore he was able to 'buy immunity from stigma' (McCormack 2012: 50) through other means. Tom played basketball, a sport associated with urban masculinities in particular (Atencio and Wright 2008). In addition to this, Tom grew up in London, meaning he spoke with vocal codes that referenced cultural signifiers of 'tougher' urban masculinities, and his Filipino heritage marked him as visibly different from his white peers (both in the focus group and in the school context more broadly). In the context of Norfolk, Tom's non-whiteness coupled with his 'urban' London background anchored his masculinity as 'tougher' and thus more appropriate and more resilient to accusations of homosexuality (see Frosh, Phoenix and Pattman 2002). Thus, although Tom was a boy who transgressed masculinity on a number of occasions, his hegemonic masculinity was never really in doubt.

When it came to those taste subjectivities and articulations which held the possibility of transgressing the masculine expectations of boys, such transgressions were rare. Any potential transgressions were reined-in in order to fit within the dominant discourses of (hegemonic) masculinity. We have seen that boys are regulated at both ends of the spectrum, both for being too masculine and not masculine enough. Homophobia remains a central regulatory force in high schools, with boys fearful of being labelled gay. As I will discuss below, this is not something that I found to be experienced by girls, demonstrating the ways in which boys experience gendered taste subjectivities very differently to girls.

Girls and Gender Inappropriate Taste

One of the main things I found in the taste cultures of participants who presented as female was that they regularly articulated tastes that were considered appropriate for boys. This follows the findings of Diane Reay, who noted in her study of primary age tomboys that 'there was an assumption, among the boys that maleness, if not a superior subject positioning, was a more desirable one' (2001: 161). In each of the focus groups there was at least one girl who not only demonstrated her preference for masculine texts, but was keen to (distancing herself from feminine subjectivities in the process). Notably though, unlike in Reay's study, none of these girls described themselves as boys, nor did they present themselves as particularly 'tomboyish' per se (all displayed markers of traditional femininity, such as long hair and most wore feminine jewellery). I am going to talk about these girls, Anna (Outskirts High), Leticia (City High, Group One), Melark (Girls High) and Naomi (City High, Group Two), and their tastes in greater depth below, but what is worth highlighting now is that such taste positions were relatively commonplace for girls (much more so than they were for boys). As such, questions are raised about whether or not these articulations can be considered to transgress gender or not, given that femininity seems to matter much less to girls than masculinity does to boys. The brief case studies provided below demonstrate what Reay has termed the '"complex relations of complicity, tension and opposition" in relation to the nexus of gender discourses that these girls draw on (2001: 156).

Anna

Anna is a particularly complicated case study in that she identifies heavily with football fandom (masculine) and has a love of Disney films (feminine), and her chosen pseudonym 'Anna' is taken from her love of the film *Anastasia* (1997). In conversations about her tastes and cultural practices she switches seamlessly between these two highly gendered taste subjectivities. Similarly, as is the case with Naomi (below), Anna repeatedly emphasised her love of football, displaying significant cultural capital with respect to the local premiership team in the process. Meanwhile, Anna also displayed 'laddish' aspects to her behaviour, making a – what seemed purposeful – slip of the tongue, calling television programme *RudeTube* (E4 2008 – present) 'RedTube' (a well-known online porn hub).

Leticia

Leticia often joined in conversations with the boys in her group, displaying capital about the texts that they were talking about, such as *The Walking Dead* (AMC 2010 – present) and male tennis players, and aligning with their verbal rejections of the (female-focused) television programme *Loose Women* (ITV 1999 – present). Leticia was the most outspoken member of the group and, at times, her attempts to gain masculine approval through her display of capital were met with rolling eyes from male and female peers alike. Leticia was also quick to mock girls that displayed try-hard masculine tastes (see below).

Melark

In the all-girl context of Girls High, Melark often positioned herself in opposition to the more feminine tastes of her peers. She readily rejected romance texts, saying 'I don't really watch that much romance films I just think they're so overrated and stereotypical I'm like, erm, more horror and humour, but not like really bad horror but funny horror like *Hot Fuzz*' (Session One), and stating that her favourite film was *Alien vs. Predator* (2004). It was clear from the discussions that Melark liked to be 'different' from her peers and, while they were sometimes intrigued by her tastes, they were never really rendered problematic. If anything, Melark appeared to gain an air of respect, and seemed a little 'cooler' than her more feminine peers.

Naomi

As with Anna, Naomi regularly switched from her highly feminine fangirling of One Direction to her developed display of football knowledge. Naomi often bemoaned her male counterparts for having not even seen all of the games of the Euro 2012 tournament taking place at the time of the focus groups. However, unlike the other girls that fell into this more transgressive category, Naomi said that she often felt ostracised for her tastes, being rendered 'too feminine' for liking One Direction and 'too masculine' for knowing so much about football.

Little Resistances?

All of the girls outlined above overemphasised their preference for masculine tastes, suggesting that this is something outside of the norm. For example, when Naomi and Anna repeated their fandom of football, they indicated that they knew that this was not a 'normal' articulation for girls such as themselves to make. In reiterating their preferences they were likely compensating for the dominant discourses of 'football' as masculine and thus primarily appropriate for boys. However, in considering the extent to which such tastes can be considered transgressive, it is worth noting that young people found means of reading potentially problematic tastes in ways that do not transgress or trouble discourses of femininity. In such instances girls' tastes are trivialised (by boys and girls alike), and the claiming of power that is associated with masculinity is renounced:

> Eliza: Well if you're a girl trying to get known with boys, on an attraction level then the whole knowing the sport would be, if you can talk about football I can see you've got loads of, obviously it doesn't always work for some people.
> [Anna pinches her, group laughs]
> (Outskirts High, Session Two)[3]

The complexity of gender is demonstrated here because, while the participants generally devalue the feminine, we can see that in this instance it is still used in the sense-making of girls' tastes (even when potentially transgressive). Based on the time that I spent with them, I think that both Anna and Naomi would be upset that their tastes could be dismissed as a means of getting a boyfriend. Such comments nevertheless suggest that a girl's preference for something masculine such as (men's) football is read as suspicious and thus not wholly accepted in terms of the dominant discourses of gender. What Eliza's reasoning (above) achieves is the reconceptualisation of gender appropriate taste in line with the dominant patriarchal discourses, and thus the claiming of power through association with masculinity is stifled.

The regulation of girls' tastes does occur then, but takes place via subtle means. Under patriarchy this serves to maintain the gender hierarchy by (re)placing authentic masculinity as out-of-bounds for girls. The ability of

Living on the Edge

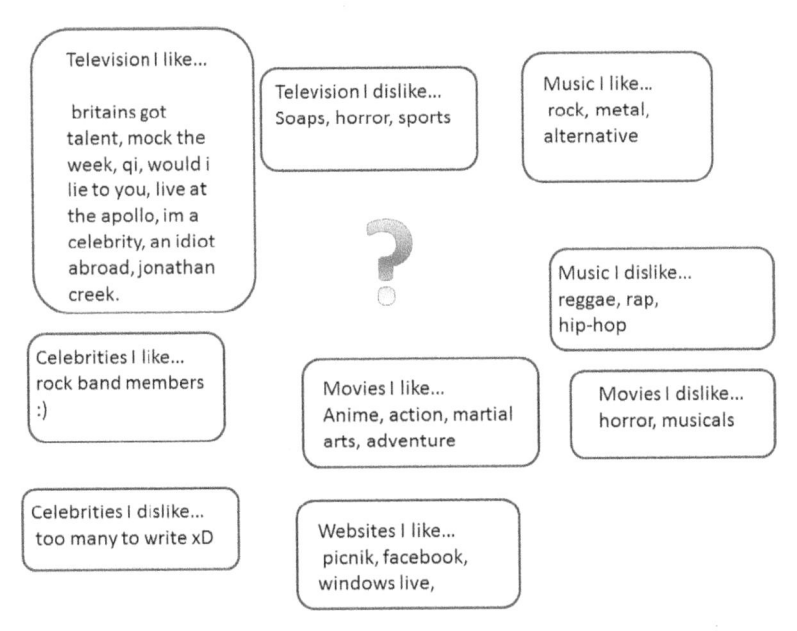

Television I like...
britains got talent, mock the week, qi, would i lie to you, live at the apollo, im a celebrity, an idiot abroad, jonathan creek.

Television I dislike...
Soaps, horror, sports

Music I like...
rock, metal, alternative

Music I dislike...
reggae, rap, hip-hop

Celebrities I like...
rock band members :)

Movies I like...
Anime, action, martial arts, adventure

Movies I dislike...
horror, musicals

Celebrities I dislike...
too many to write xD

Websites I like...
picnik, facebook, windows live,

Figure 6.3 Prompt 8

girls to claim power through identification with masculine taste articulations therefore has its limits. Examples of this can be seen in a conversation that took place during the 'Matching-Up Exercise', where it was revealed that one of the prompt-writers (who articulated a preference for a number of masculine texts – see Figure 6.3) described herself as female:

In this instance, participants problematised the prompt-writer's tastes as a 'try-hard' attempt to 'get down with the boys', and they were thus read as inappropriate. This further demonstrates some of the ways in which transgressions in girls' tastes can be discursively regulated by some of the group members, despite giving the appearance that they are all-accepting of girls' tastes.

Furthermore, when discussing the tastes of prompt-writer five (who identified with a range of masculine taste subjectivities such as liking horror, thriller and adventure films and disliking romance films), Leticia commented that she thought this person could be female, but disparaged her tastes for being too masculine:

Leticia: ... I think it's a girl that thinks she's kind of into boy things.
Erica: Yeah!
Reuben: Yeah! She thinks she's into boy things.
Leticia: Yeah but actually, reality check!
Erica: She's trying to seem cool or something.
Pedro: Reality check, sister!

(City High, Group One, Session Four)

Through the use of humour, girls' infringement on masculine subjectivities, and their associated claims to power, have been rendered problematic. In the above conversation we can see that tastes can only be rendered problematic if there *are* discourses of gender appropriate taste, and in moments such as these we can see how these discourses are (re)produced. Unlike with McGuffey and Rich's (1999) findings, we can see here that boys did not 'patrol' girls' presence in the boys' domain, but rather it was both boys *and* girls who did the patrolling. Furthermore, we see Leticia take centre stage in ridiculing the imagined girl, despite being one of the group members who routinely articulated preferences for texts with masculine value (see above). The focus group participants discussed the cultural value of 'boys' things', theorising that the imagined girl would be aligning herself alongside them to 'appear cool'. In making these claims, the discourses that normalise an understanding of the masculine as being culturally valuable are (re)produced. Thus while Halberstam (1998) or Paechter (2006) may argue that girls should avoid femininity and align themselves with masculinity because that is where power lies under patriarchy, this is much trickier to achieve in girls' lived-realities.

On the whole girls *could* make masculine taste articulations without their gender identity as 'girls' being placed under scrutiny (as may be the case for boys), but their masculine tastes could nevertheless be scrutinised on the grounds of gender appropriateness. In any of these cases it seems that gender inappropriate tastes held by girls would probably not lead them to be shunned, as the case may be with boys. I also found no accusations of girls with masculine tastes being labelled 'lesbian', something that has been found when girls transgress the rules of gender appropriateness in relation to the body (McGrath and Chananie-Hill 2009). Given the conflation between gender and sexuality detailed in Chapter 3, I found that the girls who displayed potentially problematic tastes were not labelled gay, demonstrating a notable distinction between the ways in which taste cultures are experienced by boys and girls.

One of the reasons participants gave for this increased freedom in taste articulation was that girls were imagined to have much closer and more inclusive friendship circles as compared to their male counterparts. However, feminine discourses of 'girls as caring' are employed in such moments, doing very little to trouble the dominant (patriarchal) discourses of gender. Furthermore, the space in which I found girls experienced the most freedom was at Girls High, where boys were not a part of their everyday lives. This suggests that boys play a highly regulatory role in girls' everyday cultural experiences.

Troubling?

Because these gender inappropriate taste articulations were made so often, I question the extent to which they can be considered transgressive at all. It seemed to me that there were relatively few ramifications for expressing masculine tastes if presenting as female. While a girl may be ridiculed for 'trying to be cool' by aligning herself with masculinity, this seemed to be less about her femininity being 'wrong' and more about her fraudulent attempt to claim the power of masculinity conferred by the texts with masculine value. This has much broader implications for the potential power of girls and the value of femininity under patriarchy. It appears that girls quickly learn and internalise the patriarchal devaluation of the feminine. This makes the moments of the embrace of the feminine all the more important, and all the more political, because in such moments girls (and boys or queer and non-binary youth) are acting with the knowledge that the feminine has lesser value, and yet aligning with and embracing it anyway.

Fangirling as Resistance?

We could arguably read the queering of the gender order into moments where girls actively embrace the feminine, choosing to reject patriarchal values of gender expression. This, of course, is complicated; women and girls are rewarded for adequately performing femininity with all of its classed dimensions (Skeggs 1997), while I have argued in this work that boys are shunned for aligning with femininity in most instances. The claims that I have made about how gender appropriateness operates in youth taste cultures indicate that alignment with femininity is much more transgressive for boys than it is for girls. Nevertheless it is reasonable to suggest that girls too can trouble the gendered hierarchy through close alignment with and the embrace of femininity. As I have argued in greater depth elsewhere, fangirling offers a useful example of this (see Cann 2015).

Fangirling, or the hyper-fandom of texts inscribed with feminine value (like the band One Direction), can be seen to offer contestation and negotiation to the patriarchal gender order as it rejects the discursively dominant values awarded to masculinity and femininity. While the term is often used pejoratively by young people (evidenced in this study as well as in online uses of the term (see Cann 2015: 166)), the performance of 'fangirling' (which can be enacted by any person of any age or gender) offers a unique example of the queering of the dominant gender order. This is because fangirling gives young people a means of engaging with femininity in a way which subverts patriarchal systems of value in highly visible ways. It is therefore my claim that to acknowledge the lesser value of femininity, and yet to performatively over-align with it, is something that troubles the established patriarchal value ascribed to femininity, and can therefore be considered a political act.

Concluding Remarks

On the whole, I found very little de-stabilisation of the gender hierarchy and gendered norms through taste articulation in contemporary youth culture. Boys were restrained by discourses of hegemonic masculinity and girls experienced freedom as a result of the lesser value of femininity. Even in moments of what could be read as transgressive, these discourses were rarely troubled. This is because the readings of transgressive tastes were often recuperated within dominant discourses. Participants of all genders routinely devalued what was understood to be feminine and the taste articulations of girls were rarely taken seriously enough to have an impact on a girl's social standing. Girls didn't generally need strategies to articulate preference for texts with masculine value in the same way that boys were expected to negotiate with femininity.

However, this freedom experienced by girls must be understood critically, as it is only able to be enjoyed because femininity holds such little value in contemporary youth culture(s). For boys, this was not the case, with their tastes much more rigidly constrained by ideas of what is or is not gender appropriate. Participants had a clear sense of what has masculine value and what does not, and through this hegemonic masculinity was foregrounded. Importantly, though, this was not straightforward, as aligning with 'too much' masculinity was also read as problematic.

As I have argued in Chapter 3, the increasing representation of non-cisnormative gender identities in popular culture will start to go some way in eroding the rigidity of the gender binary and, with it, notions of gender appropriate taste. While it was easier to read the queering of gender through boys taste cultures, in part due to the pervasiveness of the hegemonically masculine gender order, alternative conceptions of how 'queer' may operate in girls' taste cultures has been considered.

What I have shown in this chapter are the nuanced ways in which gender is (re)produced in contemporary youth taste cultures. The articulation of taste is experienced differently for those who present as boys and those who present as girls, and this is not only due to ideas of masculinity and femininity, but also to the socio-cultural *value* that these masculinities and femininities are seen to hold. In the patriarchal context of youth, both boys and girls continue to devalue the feminine and, only rarely, in performative instances such as fangirling, do we see young people (overwhelmingly girls) embracing femininity. Texts with masculine value however were something that both boys and girls could articulate a preference for, and this is, I propose, because masculinity confers value under patriarchy. The hyper-regulatory space of high school therefore (re)produces gender, as notions of gender inappropriate tastes mark the boundaries of who and what young people can be when it comes to gender.

Conclusions and Recommendations

What does gender mean for young people and what role does it play in their everyday experiences? Is youth really a site where 'prevailing ideas about identity and status are questioned, suspended or reversed' (Hesmondhalgh 2005: 37), or is it much more rigid than that? Youth has, for a long time, been romanticised as a distinctively unruly and subversive period of our cultural lives, in both academic work and popular culture more widely, but what I have uncovered in this book is that young people are much more hesitant to trouble the dominant order than one might assume. The gender binary, and all that comes with it, is stubbornly persistent, and offers very little to young people other than a series of discourses which produce narrow subjectivities. This is not to say that queer and non-binary youth are not out there in the UK, far from it, but rather that these young people are brave; brave due to their very existence challenging the dominant gender discourses in the hyper-regulatory context of high school.

The patriarchal discourses which produce these narrow parameters of gender serve not only to devalue the feminine (and by association the tastes of girls), but also to do significant harm to boys. The fragility of masculinity is readily evidenced in the discussions held during the course of this study. Calling this book *Girls Like This: Boys Like That* speaks directly to the notion held by these young people that girls' and boys' tastes are highly distinct and, through fear of homosexualisation, boys simply cannot 'like' the same sorts of things that girls do. Rather depressingly, we see in youth taste cultures a clear example of the feminine as 'Other', operating as readily today as in the time of de Beauvoir's writing on *The Second Sex* (1972 [1949]). It is my contention that these patriarchal discourses harm boys as much as they do girls, that their regulatory function does little other than to limit who and what young people can be, limiting their future possibilities as much as their current ones.

Through examination of the literature I have found that youth taste is a vastly underexplored field, but through empirical investigation I have shown that it is also an incredibly rich one for academic exploration. Young people's discussions about taste may appear mundane and inconsequential, but they are not. Not only can we learn much about from the everydayness of youth taste cultures, but importantly we can see the central role that youth taste cultures play in the (re)production of identity. Because youth taste cultures are regulatory spaces, through their examination we are able to develop an understanding of how discursively 'regular' identities are (re)produced through taste articulation. This book has focused on the intersection of gender and youth, but the framework that I have developed can certainly be used to investigate the (re)production of other identities (and their intersection(s)), and I would encourage further work to do so; taking seriously the role that taste plays in people's cultural lives.

Youth Taste Cultures and Hyper-Regulation

Youth taste cultures are at the heart of this book and they are a central space where young people work out what subjectivities they can (re)produce. In my account of the field of youth studies I have argued that scholars, for many years now, have been interested in the cultural lives of young people. Many of these scholars have interrogated young people's consumption practices (see Bennett 2011 for a useful overview of this); however a surprisingly low number of these studies have examined their taste cultures more specifically. One of the contributions that this book makes to this body of knowledge then is in highlighting the significance of youth taste cultures as a site of identity (re)production. Within taste culture theory, much of the literature has followed in the footsteps of Pierre Bourdieu's now iconic *Distinction*, displaying a particular interest in the reproduction of class identities through distinctions in taste.

In these analyses of taste cultures gender has been largely absent (with the work of Beverley Skeggs (1997, 2004b) providing a notable exception). This book has therefore sought to place gender firmly within our

Conclusions and Recommendations

understanding of the socio-cultural function of taste. Through empirical investigation I have found that young people draw on discourses of gender in order to render some cultural texts appropriate or inappropriate for someone to like (or not) on the grounds of gendered expectations. All cultural texts can have gender inscribed into them, and can thus be collectively understood to mean something to a person of a particular gender. As a social phenomenon this can help us to explain how ideas of gender appropriateness function within everyday culture. The findings in this book clearly demonstrate that taste cultures *are* experienced differently by those of different genders, and that tastes can be rendered (in)appropriate on the grounds of gender too. It is my hope that this book will inspire future cultural theorists, audience studies scholars and sociologists to undertake interrogations into the (re)production of a range of identities and their dynamics of power through taste articulation and within taste cultures (not least race, (dis)ability and generation).

Bethany Bryson (1996) has argued that much of the contemporary taste culture literature has focused on the things that people like, rather than those that they do not. I have addressed this by ensuring that the things young people disliked were given as much focus as those they said they liked. The outcome of this was significant as it appeared there were a number of gender appropriate *dislikes* for young people, especially with respect to boys saying they dislike feminine texts. This finding was available because I built a holistic approach to taste into my methodological approach, and thus I urge future scholars of taste cultures to do the same.

Having knowledge of what is gender appropriate or inappropriate to like is crucial to young people at high school because not liking the 'right' thing can lead to the questioning of one's gendered subjectivity. This is particularly crucial for boys, because if a boy were to say he liked something feminine, such as a classic romantic comedy like *Pretty Woman* (1990), then he would run the 'risk' of being called gay – something that remains problematic in the largely homophobic space of high school. It is important to reiterate that the participants believed that being in high school was central to why they felt so restricted, following my claim that high school is a hyper-regulatory space. Understanding high school to be hyper-regulatory is significant because this is what makes gender appropriate articulations so necessary to young people's everyday experiences of taste and cultural consumption, particularly in terms of the gendered parameters of appropriateness.

Hyper-Regulation

As suggested above, one of the reasons that taste cultures were found to provide such an important role during youth was because of the hyper-regulatory space of high school (and this is a result of the high number of young people spending long periods of time alongside one another in a confined space, with repetitive daily routines and movement in cohorts). In Chapter 2, I analysed the empirical findings to reveal *why* taste mattered in youth culture, and through this I showed that young people are all too aware of the consequences of inappropriate performances. When the tastes of a young person are rendered gender inappropriate they risk being 'shunned'. I have argued that the use of the word 'shunned' is a useful one for thinking about discursive regulation, and for this reason suggest it should be integrated more fully into the youth studies vocabulary. The word 'shunned' (used by the young people interviewed in this study) can help us to understand the consequences of failing to (re)produce gender appropriate taste(s). It describes a collective form of social rejection and so is useful for describing the processes that I either witnessed happening (during the course of the focus groups and exploratory ethnography), or that the participants described as having experienced. When asked to talk about how and when shunning occurs, those at Outskirts High provided examples which included both physical and verbal forms of punishment, with 'spreading it' being seen as the worst. In many ways, the threat of being shunned provided a panopticon style form of self-regulation amongst young people at high school. Fear of being shunned therefore provides motivation to perform gender appropriate taste in a context that is hyper-regulatory.

Taste and the (Re)Production of Gender

Young people who present as male and who present as female *do* experience taste cultures differently. Boys' tastes are much more heavily regulated than girls' tastes, and this is largely because masculinity and femininity are understood as having very different socio-cultural values.

Conclusions and Recommendations

Taste articulations were often rendered inappropriate on the grounds of gendered expectations, and feminine texts were largely devalued across gender groups.

I think it would be fair to say that a common theme across the findings presented in this book is the lack of straightforwardness when it comes to the role of gender in youth taste cultures. In disconnecting masculinity from being inherently about maleness, and femininity from inherent femaleness, I have been able to show how young people discursively (re)produce gender and its subjectivities. In asking questions about what is feminine and what is masculine, alongside what boys and girls *do* with this, I have been able to show how young people negotiate the parameters of gender. This research therefore develops work by Becky Francis (2008, 2010a) and Carrie Paechter (2006, 2007, 2012) who have argued that there has been a conflation not only between sex and gender but also between gender and gender expression within academic research. Rather than simply assuming that girls' tastes are automatically *feminine* tastes, I have been able to offer an account of young people's gendered experiences. What I have found to be significant is that in youth taste culture the gender one is attributed is the gender which one's tastes must 'match'. Under patriarchy this is particularly important for boys. The reasons for this are twofold; in the first instance the masculine is seen as having *value* (across genders), and the second reason is that boys are discursively associated with masculinity, such that it is boys who have more to lose by distancing themselves from it. Comparatively, when it came to girls' lives and their tastes, much greater fluidity was demonstrated. However, the cost of this is the discursive devaluation of the feminine. Thus, one of the strengths of examining youth taste cultures is that they offer a space where we can see the complexities of these relationships.

In the context of boys' taste cultures, hegemonic masculinities were the most appropriate and unproblematic gender subjectivities for boys to perform. There were a range of cultural texts that boys could either align or dis-align with that would allow boys to perform an appropriate hegemonic masculinity. Cultural texts tended to be seen as appropriate for boys to like if they held the proponents of hegemonic masculinity, namely foregrounding physicality and heterosexuality (Connell 2005). But of course, boys' tastes were much more complicated than that, and while hegemonic masculinity was certainly the form considered most appropriate, it was also the case that 'too much' of it could be rendered problematic. Within this book I have drawn on empirical evidence to show that hegemonic masculinity certainly occupies a complex position in the lives of boys (and indeed girls) and, while Connell's hegemonic masculinity theory posits that the properties of physicality and heterosexuality (amongst others) are desirable, this research has demonstrated that such desirability is limited. My empirical analysis has showed the significance of hegemonic masculinity in the appropriate taste articulations of boys, but also that this relationship is far from straightforward, and nor is it easily and/or readily taken up.

Looking specifically at issues of boys' tastes, and of masculinity, the findings in this book contribute to the lively debates that are taking place within contemporary masculinity studies (see Haywood and Mac an Ghaill 2012; Roberts 2014 for overviews). In my exploration of the existing works in these fields, I discussed how hegemonic masculinity studies theorists have found their work under increasing scrutiny from proponents of inclusive masculinity. This is the part of my book where I should probably nail my colours to the mast in terms of this debate. Can I say that it is complicated? Certainly the take up of hegemonic masculinity was not straightforward in the cases that I saw in the course of this research, but I certainly would not feel comfortable describing the hyper-regulatory context of the high schools that I was at as operating as a space of inclusive masculinity. I have found that there is *potential* for boys to have a more fluid relationship with masculinity and their performance of it. However, I also found that due to the fear of being shunned, this potential was almost never realised. While some boys discussed how 'being yourself' and thus 'honest' about what you say you like was possible in certain contexts with close friends, there was nevertheless a clear sense held by all of them of what was 'publicly' acceptable to articulate in terms of taste. For this reason, transgressions of gender appropriateness in taste were rarely achieved. We can make sense of this lack of transgression through the ways in which the sexuality label 'gay' was often conflated with instances of non-traditionally masculine subjectivities being performed by boys. I have suggested that the label of 'gay', while not *entirely* problematic, was one that boys who were not gay were very keen to avoid. Fear of being homosexualised therefore allows us to see that the young people in this study are located in a context that inclusive masculinity theorist Eric

Conclusions and Recommendations

Anderson may describe as 'homohysteric' (2009: 95). Fear of being labelled 'gay', therefore, reveals much about how and why it is that I have found the pervasiveness of hegemonic masculinity within the experiences of taste cultures for boys, particularly in terms of what is and is not collectively deemed 'gender appropriate'.

When it comes to the analysis of girls' tastes both masculinities and femininities were negotiated in highly complex ways. And thus, while not straightforward, I have argued that girls' taste cultures are complicated for different reasons than boys'. In terms of what were considered appropriate tastes for girls I found that almost anything 'goes'. I posit this because girls, in their presented and attributed female gender, are understood as those for whom femininity is deemed appropriate. However, I found that the feminine has very little value within contemporary youth taste cultures, which is perhaps unsurprising under patriarchy. This devaluation of the feminine has given girls considerable freedom when it comes to the expression of taste as, generally speaking, these girls have very little symbolic power to lose. That said, it is not simply the case that girls rejected the lesser value of the feminine, nor did they see it as especially valuable either.

Traditional concepts of femininity were drawn upon when describing the properties of texts that were seen as *most* appropriate for girls to like. Texts that represented love and romance were often the ones which participants discussed as being valuable to girls – and simultaneously inappropriate for boys. However, on the whole, the girls who articulated preferences for these sorts of texts tended to describe them as a 'guilty pleasure', and many of the girls rejected them on the grounds that they were seen to have little value. Unlike with texts that had masculine value, outside of the texts that represented romance, few cultural texts were understood as having feminine value. I have argued that this is because the feminine is generally not described as having wider cultural value during youth. Instead, I noted that the feminine was less about the texts themselves and more about the *means* of articulating taste. As part of this I have been able to argue that it is important to examine not only what is liked or disliked in youth taste cultures but also *how* these tastes are articulated. For example, I found that 'bitching' was considered central to the assumption that girls are interested in celebrity culture; meanwhile 'fangirling' offered girls a means of performing excessive femininities while troubling the patriarchal devaluation of the feminine in the process. This raises a range of questions about the role of *articulation* in taste cultures, not least in understanding the (re)production of gender. It seemed to me that despite appearing diverse, a clear understanding of femininity in girls' tastes was nevertheless (re)produced.

This research has therefore revealed that although femininity may address the qualities of being female (Thomas 2008), what is acceptable for girls is much broader than just the 'feminine'. At various intervals girls 'appropriately' articulated preferences for masculine texts, and furthermore many girls said they disliked a wide range of feminine texts. Girls are therefore able to articulate tastes in the same way as their male peers, but boys were found to be significantly more regulated than girls. These findings show that youth taste cultures are spaces where girls can potentially perform masculine subjectivities, further contributing to the understanding of female masculinities that has been developed in recent years (Francis 2010a; Halberstam, 1998; Paechter 2006; Renold 2007). Thus while boys' tastes are discursively regulated on the ground of appropriateness, the same cannot be said for girls. In thinking about how broad girls' tastes have been found to be within the empirical evidence collected in this book, we can come to better understand how the term 'girl' has come to be so slippery and indeterminate (as Harris 2004b describes). The subordinate position which femininity occupies in relation to masculinity therefore makes is less than desirable to align with, demonstrating the pervasive work that patriarchy does in girls' everyday lives.

Reflections and Future Research

When I started this research, I did not know what I would find, but I did know that I wanted the voices and experiences of young people to be at the forefront of my work. The methods that I have developed and employed within the course of this three-year project demonstrate my commitment to this end, and I am proud that my research has been tailored to the specificities of the youth experience. Through this I feel I have been able to capture at least some of the richness of young people's cultural lives.

By using identity pages as prompts in the focus group discussions, I was able to ensure that the participants were responding to the 'real' tastes of people their age. In Group One at City High Leticia even commented that

Conclusions and Recommendations

she could tell I hadn't made them up myself because the tastes given were so subtle and thus 'realistic'. Use of digital media therefore offers great potential in empirical youth studies research, particularly when combined with traditional methodologies such as focus groups. I hope that future researchers take inspiration from the richness of data that I have collected here and employ similar methods in the future.

There are, however, limitations to this research. In the process of undertaking this study I have been forced to focus on particular areas and not others. A benefit of this is that I have been able to develop this rich understanding of gender and youth taste cultures, but this also means that there are absences and invisibilities in this research – particularly in terms of intersectional identities. In acknowledging these absences I show the need for the consideration of intersectional identities within future research. Despite a relatively diverse black and minority ethnic sample (in relation to the geography of the investigation), I have chosen not to elucidate issues of race. Similarly, I have not reflected on class and, given class's centrality within studies of taste, this may be considered a weakness within my research. Beverley Skeggs (1997) has shown what insight can be garnered from a focus on gender and class when looking at taste, but my research has never sought to mirror that of Skeggs. My research questions were instead focused around questions of gender more specifically, seeking to uncover the complexities of gender within contemporary youth taste cultures. Undoubtedly class plays a central role in how taste is experienced; the countless studies that have followed in the footsteps of Pierre Bourdieu have found this to be the case. I hope that I have demonstrated well enough why I have chosen to focus on gender instead of class in this work. It is not the case that I believe class or race (or any other social identity) are less important than gender or age, but rather that I think they are categories that are too significant to mention only tangentially. I propose that to mention them while not really grappling with their complexities would be to the detriment not only of my research, but also of the complexities of these identities.[1] There is great scope for future research to interrogate these intersectional identities (including class, race, (dis)ability, sexuality and so forth) in relation to taste cultures, and I urge such work to be undertaken, not simply to allay criticisms that my work does not do this, but because such work is urgent and necessary.

Reifying the Gender Binary?

I have analysed gender and youth taste cultures from a poststructuralist perspective, attempting to queer accounts of gender in the process. Ros Gill has argued that in poststructuralist theory meaning is 'fluid, ambiguous and contradictory' (2007: 13), highlighting one of the difficulties of applying this perspective within empirical research. However, just because meaning is not fixed, it can nevertheless be temporarily stabilised. What I have shown in this book is that through the gendering of particular taste articulations an understanding of what gender *is* and *means* is (temporarily) fixed for young people. Presenting these empirical findings has been challenging, as, following Francis, categorising different behaviours/tastes/texts as gendered runs the risk of reifying the gender binary in the process (2010a: 478). I am constrained not only by the inherent gendering of the English language, but also by the need to 'fix', if only temporarily, my analysis of gender onto the pages of this book. I hope that in my discussion of 'boyness' and 'girlness', masculinity and femininity, I have been able to stay true to this poststructuralist position as much as possible. I have shown, I hope, that masculinity and femininity are ideas and expressions which can be picked up by anybody, and be performed by anybody. However, I have shown that, despite this potential for transgression, young people rarely do actually trouble gender, and this is at least in part because they are fearful of being shunned within the hyper-regulatory space of high school.

Although all of the focus group participants presented as cisgender, and their expression of gender matched their presentation of gender, it is my belief that the theories developed here could certainly be applied to trans, non-binary and queer young people. In the case of queer youth the examination of taste and how the articulation of taste can trouble the gender binary would provide a fascinating site for further study and I thus wholeheartedly encourage such work to be undertaken. Similarly, an investigation with trans youth could help us to understand how taste articulation can also fix gender for this group of young people. Furthermore, questions are raised about the extent to which rejections of the feminine can be considered a cis-girl's privilege.

As a feminist researcher I am both grateful that we have a better understanding of how the feminine continues to have a lesser value within youth cultures, and disheartened to find that patriarchal discourses persevere in the current day. There is a need for further investigation into how the feminine is devalued in discussions of taste and cultural consumption. Because femininity is associated with girls, this connects those who are attributed the identity of 'girl' with a lower cultural position. Is it any wonder that so many girls (and boys) rejected things that are associated with femininity when femininity is seen to confer such little value? This book therefore provides empirical evidence to support Carrie Paechter's claim that distancing oneself from the feminine is about the claiming of power (2006: 257). In light of this I am keen to develop a richer understanding of the devaluation of the feminine, particularly as there were some moments where participants embraced the hyper-feminine through acts of fangirling. In such moments, the complexity of gendered value is raised, and we are given reasons for further interrogation of the role that femininity plays within youth taste cultures.

Potential for Change? Recommendations and Cultural Sensitivities

Following a focus group held at City High, one of the participants, Naomi, asked me what I wanted to do or achieve with the research. I told her that I hoped to better understand what it's like to be a teenager and maybe make life a little bit easier for those that didn't really fit in. Naomi, someone who had routinely been teased for her tastes, told me that she thought it would be really hard to change those sorts of behaviours. This final section then is in part, a response to Naomi, with the hope that we can achieve some socio-cultural changes to make life a little nicer for people like her.

Changes in School

If compulsory schooling is to be enforced (indeed as I believe it should be to ensure equality of access to education), then we must be sensitive to the hyper-regulation that takes place on school grounds. Many British high schools have a commitment to developing student confidence at the heart of their mission statements. This research has found that many young people simply do not have the confidence to say what they really think, and to be fully open with their peers. Such self-regulation motivated by fear of being shunned can have long-term effects on the healthy emotional development of these young people into their adult years. The findings from this research can therefore reveal that perhaps schools are not adequately meeting the aims of their mission statements.

With this in mind I propose the following changes which schools could implement to help improve the gendered experiences of their pupils.[2] There are also clearly classed and raced dimensions to how taste is regulated and experienced at high school, and thus the recommendations made here should also speak to other intersecting identities.

- Devote time at staff meetings and teacher training events to discussing student confidence and to identifying problem areas.
- David, Ringrose and Showunmi describe the content of subjects that provide space for engagement with issues of gender equality, such as Citizenship, Personal, Social and Health Education (PSHE) and Sex and Relationships Education (SRE), as 'opaque to say the least' (2010: 8). This must change if we are to encourage intercultural dialogue, cultural sensitivity and peer-to-peer respect. Schools therefore need to invest in the development of these subjects – ideally in conversation with students themselves – as a means of making these subjects relevant, timely and valuable to the student cohort.

Changes in Government Policy

Marshall writes that theories and methods need to be integrated with the realities of power, and thus '[i]ntegrating feminist and critical theory into policy analysis will add critical issues and ways of framing questions about power, justice and the state' (1997: 2). We therefore require not only changes to government policy, but also the fostering of greater feminist interrogation of policy, particularly in areas which can have a profound impact on the development of gender norms.

- Government funding must be made available for teachers to attend training and events provided by organisations such as Gendered Intelligence.[3]

Conclusions and Recommendations

- Curriculum content must reward 'softer' subjects that promote cultural sensitivities such as PSHE, SRE and Citizenship, so that they are not lost in the cracks of GCSE targets.
- The 'bonfire of the quangos' in 2010 saw British politics lose its 'gender duty' which required gender audits of policy, and this has arguably been to the detriment of wider gender equality. Commitment to the equality of opportunity on the basis of gender remains crucial should we hope to achieve fairness.

Final Remarks

The politics of taste is fundamental to how we understand the discursive (re)production of identity. Persistent inequality is experienced on the grounds of identity (sexism, racism, homophobia and ableism to name just a few), and through the interrogation of taste cultures we are able to uncover the everyday ways in which these differences are (re)produced. This research, like much other audience research, is so important because it renders 'problematic taken-for-granted ideas and beliefs circulating in society about gender' (Carter and Steiner 2004: 28). Through this research it is my hope that I inspire future cultural studies, sociology and audience studies research to examine taste cultures, as this book has shown its usefulness for examining these taken-for-granted ideals.

My motivation has been not only to develop an understanding of the role which taste plays in the (re)production of gender (a much overlooked field within the academic literature), but also to develop our understanding of why gender persists as a cultural category in and of itself. The richness of the empirical evidence that has been collected in this research has allowed me to develop this understanding. This book has demonstrated the importance of considering the role that gender plays in experiences of taste. I am not saying that gender is the only, nor indeed even the *most*, important element in discourses of appropriate taste, but what I *am* claiming is that we must not overlook the integral role that gender plays in how young people negotiate their taste cultures, both individually and collectively. When young people talk about the things that they like or dislike, they (re)produce gender. Gender is regulated within contemporary youth taste cultures because discourses of gender appropriate taste remind young people of the parameters of what articulations are permissible.

I have shown that because school is a hyper-regulatory space, and because young people fear being shunned, they have the motivation to articulate appropriate taste. I hope that this is the first in a long line of research that considers the role of taste in the (re)production of gender, unravelling the discourses that hold them together and producing new, accepted, gendered subjectivities in the process.

Notes

Introduction

1. Bourdieu (2010) considered gender to be a secondary category and this has therefore been noted as a significant 'blind spot' within his thesis of distinction (for further exploration see Bennett et al. 2009: 214–33; Dumais 2002; Huppatz 2009; Laberge 1995; McNay 1999; Skeggs 2004a).
2. This is before we take into account the impact and double disadvantages of intersectional identities.

1 Researching Youth Taste Cultures: The Study

1. Pupil premium is government funding for children from forces families, low-income families or children that are in care, who are eligible for free school meals or have been eligible for free school meals within the past six years (Ofsted 2012: 7).
2. At Outskirts High all of the participants were from the 'East Side' of the school except for Chloe who was the only participant from the 'West Side'.

2 Fitting in at School: The Context of Youth Taste Cultures

1. Also noteworthy is the sheer 'whiteness' of the Hollywood High School Movie, and thus, perhaps, the collective experience that is captured in these films is indeed the 'White High School Experience'.
2. For example, a girl could like Justin Bieber, even if Justin Bieber does not hold much value in the wider context of school. Indeed, as is the case with many texts

considered gender-appropriate for girls to like, the feminine is largely rendered trivial and value-less (see discussions in Chapter 5).
3. It is possible that through after-school clubs and the presence of peers on social media sites this hyper-regulation extends well beyond the parameters of the school walls.
4. It is important to note that this is what the participants think and not my own belief. I would argue that adulthood remains a highly regulated space, and some spaces may still be hyper-regulatory. It is nevertheless significant that participants made this distinction and that they imagine adulthood as less restrictive, indicating a generationally distinct experience of taste.
5. This was also one of the few times that the private school girls of Girls High explicitly distinguished themselves from their state-educated peers.
6. This also raises questions surrounding the trans and non-binary experience, in particular how this feeling of belonging is played out.

3 What is Gender? Theorising Gender and Young People's Lived Experiences

1. When I use the term 'present as' I am referring to the gender identity that is being communicated to the audience, unless a queer presentation is being given (which was not the case in any of the focus groups) – it is my belief that gender is attributed on the basis of this presentation. I want to move away from biologically deterministic accounts of gender not least because '[a]ttributions are almost always made in the absence of information about genitals' (Kessler and McKenna 1978: 17), and, following Butler (1990), what these genitals *mean* are socially constructed anyway.
2. The implication here is that to know their gender one must have *seen* their genitalia to be certain.

4 Boys Like This: Masculinity and Appropriate Tastes for Boys

1. The implication is that texts that hold masculine capital have masculine value. However, McCormack's use of the concept 'masculine capital' is not developed, limiting the extent to which we can understand *how* the masculine capital of the text 'buys' immunity from stigma. I argue instead that by aligning with texts that have masculine value (by a boy saying he likes something understood to be masculine) a masculine expression that fits the dominant discourses of masculinity is (re)produced.
2. Naomi often discussed her tastes in ways that showed she knew and acknowledged that her tastes were often more masculine than feminine, and her

love of watching football was frequently cited as an example of this. As I show in my discussions of girls' tastes, preference for texts with masculine value was not always considered inappropriate for girls as '[d]istancing oneself from stereotypical femininity [...] is a claiming of power' (Paechter 2006: 257).
3. Again, this is a very 'white' form of culture being discussed and perhaps speaks more to the *white* hegemonically masculine experience.
4. Price and Fox featured on two of the prompts used in the focus groups (Prompt 2 and Prompt 5).
5. The term 'uncanny valley' describes the dip (or valley) of comfortableness, whereby as 'robots appear more humanlike, our sense of their familiarity increases until we come to a valley' (Mori 1970: 33).

5 Girls Like That: Femininity and Appropriate Tastes for Girls

1. These discourses are also (re)produced in the *distance* seen between romance and proponents of hegemonic masculinity (emotionality in opposition to physicality). The 'femininity of romance' is thus inscribed in part through the absence of masculinity.
2. It should be noted that this is an assumption made by Phoebe and is part of her sense-making of the gendering of taste, as *90210* has always featured many male characters.
3. Anna's choice of the pronoun 'he' is noteworthy as she used it based on the taste articulations given on the prompt that she read as belonging to a boy – this belief was strengthened by the prompt-writers dislike of something feminine, romance texts.
4. This discussion also reminds us that the genderings are not fixed and can change over time. The attractiveness of The Beatles explains their appeal to girls *back then*.
5. The participants also connected Twitter to other texts that were inscribed with feminine value – such as pop acts like One Direction and Justin Bieber (further emphasising its appropriateness for girls).
6. Marmite is a spread (grocery) sold in the UK that has the tagline 'Love it/ Hate it'.
7. Given Justin Bieber's very public 'growing up' and entry into 'manhood', including public brawls, dick pics and (hetero)sex scandals it is important to note that this study took place when Bieber was still a relatively 'clean' pop star.
8. This is further complicated when we compare this to the work of Mendick et al. (2018) who have found that Katie Price's entrepreneurial skills marked her as aspirational. There are almost certainly classed elements to these two opposing readings.

6 Living on the Edge: Regulating and Transgressing Gender Appropriate Taste

1. It is not clear what would happen if a person that presented as female expressed these articulations, but my findings suggest that this would be met with similar responses. However, it may be the case that a girl is read as suspicious because she is claiming power through association with masculinity, whereas boys are met with suspicion because it is assumed that they have 'something to hide'.
2. It is worth noting that Tom's transgressions were nevertheless meaningful, particularly because they were made within the hyper-regulatory space of high school.
3. The commas here reflect on style of speech i.e. pauses in the teenager's account.

Conclusions and Recommendations

1. I am under no illusions that noting race as an area of 'invisibility' in my research is a bit of a cop out, but my position is one that wants to do justice to the identities that I interrogate (in this book, gender and age). Class and race need to be a significant focus of study and not simply given cursory mentions on the grounds of being a 'good white feminist', as giving such areas lip service offers little justice to the complex lived experiences of these intersectional identities and the discourses of oppression that they are subject to.
2. It should be noted that any changes made to school policies should be tailored to each context, as this study has revealed the importance of the distinct contexts. Furthermore good practice in this area must be shared.
3. Gendered Intelligence is a Community Interest Company that supports young trans people and aims to increase understandings of gender diversity. They are a not-for-profit company established in 2008.

Bibliography

Aapola, S., Gonick, M. and Harris, A. (2005) *Young Femininity: Girlhood, Power and Social Change*, New York: Palgrave Macmillan.

Abbott, D. (2013) 'Britain's Crisis of Masculinity: Good health, hard work and family' *A Demos Twentieth Birthday lecture delivered by Diane Abbott MP* Demos, Magdalen House, London: Demos 1–11.

Anderson, E. (2009) *Inclusive Masculinity: The Changing Nature of Masculinities*, London: Routledge.

Andersson, F. (2008) 'Constructing Young Masculinity: A case study of heroic discourse on violence' *Discourse & Society*, 19(2): 139–61.

Ang, I. (1985) *Watching Dallas: Soap Opera and the Melodramatic Imagination*, New York: Methuen.

Atencio, M. and Wright, J. (2008) '"We Be Killin' Them": Hierarchies of Black masculinity in urban basketball spaces' *Sociology of Sport Journal*, 25(2): 263–80.

Ashley, M. (2009) 'Time to Confront Willis's Lads with a Ballet Class? A case study of educational orthodoxy and white working class boys' *British Journal of Sociology of Education*, 30(2): 179–91.

—— (2011) 'The Perpetuation of Hegemonic Male Power and the Loss of Boyhood Innocence: Case studies from the music industry' *Journal of Youth Studies*, 14(1): 59–76.

Barker, G. (2005) *Dying to be Men: Youth, Masculinity and Social Exclusion*, London: Routledge.

Barry, P. (2009) *Beginning Theory: An Introduction to Literary and Cultural Theory*, Manchester: Manchester University Press.

Bates, L. (2014) *Everyday Sexism*, London: Simon & Schuster.

Baumgardner, J. and Richards, A. (2004) 'Feminism and Femininity: Or how we learned to stop worrying and love the thong' in A. Harris (ed.), *All about the Girl: Culture, Power and Identity*, New York: Routledge: 59–68.

de Beauviour, S. (1972) *The Second Sex*, Harmondsworth: Penguin.

Bennett, A. (2011) 'The Post-Subcultural Turn: Some reflections 10 years on' *Journal of Youth Studies*, 14(5): 493–506.

Bennett, T., Savage, M., Silva, E., Warde, A., Gayo-Cal, M. and Wright, D. (2009) *Culture, Class, Distinction*, London: Routledge.

Biklen, S.K. (2004) 'Trouble on Memory Lane: Adults and self-retrospection in researching youth' *Qualitative Inquiry*, 10(5): 715–30.

Blackman, S. (1998) 'Poxy Cupid! An ethnographic and feminist account of a resistant female youth culture' in T. Skelton and G. Valentine (eds), *The New Wave Girls. Cool Places: Geographies of Youth Cultures*, London: Routledge: 207–28

Boberg, M., Piippo, P. and Ollila, E. (2008) 'Designing Avatars' *3rd International Conference on Digital Interactive Entertainment and Arts. D.I.M.i.E. a. Arts*, Athens: Greece, DIMEA, 232–9.

Bourdieu, P. (2010) *Distinction: A Social Critique of the Judgement of Taste*, London: Routledge.

Brown, L.M. (1998) *Raising Their Voices: The Politics of Girls' Anger*, Cambridge: Harvard University Press.

Bryson, B. (1996) '"Anything But Heavy Metal": Symbolic exclusion and musical dislikes' *American Sociological Review*, 61(5): 884–99.

—— (1997) 'What about the Univores? Musical dislikes and group-based identity construction among Americans with low levels of education' *Poetics*, 25(2–3): 141–56.

Bulman, R.C. (2005) *Hollywood Goes to High School: Cinema, Schools and American Culture*, New York: Worth.

Butler, J. (1990) *Gender Trouble: Feminism and the Subversion of Identity*, London: Routledge.

—— (1993) *Bodies That Matter: On the Discursive Limits of 'Sex'*, London: Routledge.

—— (2004) *Undoing Gender*, New York: Routledge.

Cann, V. (2014) 'The Limits of Masculinity: Boys, taste and cultural consumption' in S. Roberts (ed.), *Debating Modern Masculinities: Change, Continuity, Crisis*, London: Palgrave Pivot. 17–34.

—— (2015) 'Girls and Cultural Consumption: "Fangirls", "typical girls" and the value of femininity' in H. Savigny and H. Warner (eds), *Gender and 21st Century Popular Culture: The Politics of being a Woman*, London: Palgrave Macmillan (pp. 154–74).

Carter, C. and Steiner, L. (2004) 'Mapping the Contested Terrain of Media and Gender Research' in C. Carter and L. Steiner (eds), *Critical Readings: Media and Gender*, Maidenhead: Open University Press: 11–36.

Cheng, C. (1999) 'Marginalized Masculinities and Hegemonic Masculinity: An introduction' *The Journal of Men's Studies*, 7(3): 295–315.

Cole, S. (2012) *Discourses of Masculinity: Culture, Identity and Violence*, Available at: http://www.inter-disciplinary.net/wp-content/uploads/2012/02/coleipaper.pdf (last accessed 18 December 2013).

Connell, R. (1987) *Gender and Power*, Cambridge: Polity Press.

—— (1995) *Masculinities*, Berkeley: University of California Press.

Bibliography

—— (2005) *Masculinities* (2nd edn), Berkeley: University of California Press.
Connell, R.W. and Messerschmidt, J.W. (2005) 'Hegemonic Masculinity: Rethinking the concept' *Gender & Society*, 19(6): 829–59.
Consalvo, M. (2003) 'The monsters Next Door: Media constructions of boys and masculinity' *Feminist Media Studies*, 3(1): 27–45.
Coy, M. and Garner, M. (2010) 'Glamour Modelling and the Marketing of Self-Sexualization: Critical reflections' *International Journal of Cultural Studies*, 13(6): 657–75.
Currie, D., Kelly, D. and Pomerantz, S. (2009) *'Girl Power': Girls Reinventing Girlhood*, New York: Peter Lang.
Dare-Edwards, H.L. (2014) '"Shipping Bullshit": Twitter rumours, fan/celebrity interaction and questions of authenticity' *Celebrity Studies*, 5(4): 521–4.
David, M., Ringrose, J., and Showunmi, V. (2010) 'Browne Report and the White Paper: A murky outlook for educational equality' *GEA Policy Report*, Available at: http://www.genderandeducation.com/wp-content/uploads/2011/01/GEA_Policy_Report_October_December_20101.pdf (accessed 30 August 2017).
Driscoll, C. (2002) *Girls: Feminine Adolescence in Popular Culture and Cultural Theory*, New York: Columbia University Press.
—— (2011) *Teen Film: A Critical Introduction*, Oxford: Berg.
Driver, S. (2008) *Queer Youth Cultures*, Albany: State University of New York Press.
Dumais, S. (2002) 'Cultural Capital, Gender and School Success: The role of habitus' *Sociology of Education*, 75(1): 44–68.
Dunbar Jr, C., Rodriguez, D. and Parker, L. (2001) 'Race, Subjectivity and the Interview Process' in J. Gubrium and J. Holstein (eds), *Handbook of Interview Research: Context and Method*, London: Sage: 279–98.
Ehrenreich, B. (2003) 'Beatlemania: Girls just want to have fun' in W. Brooker and D. Jermyn (eds), *The Audience Studies Reader*, London: Routledge: 180–4.
Epstein, D. and Johnson, R. (1998) *Schooling Sexualities*, Buckingham: Open University Press.
Evans, B. (2006) '"I'd Feel Ashamed": Girls' bodies and sports participation' *Gender, Place & Culture*, 13(5): 547–61.
Faludi, S. (1999) *Stiffed: The Betrayal of Modern Man*, London: Chatto & Windus.
Ferguson, A. (2001) *Bad Boys: Public Schools in the Making of Black Masculinity*, Ann Arbor: University of Michigan Press.
Fielding, N. (1993) 'Qualitative Interviewing' in N. Gilbert (ed.), *Researching Social Life*, London: Sage: 135–53.
Fine, C. (2010) *Delusions of Gender: The Real Science Behind Gender Differences*, London: Icon Books.
Foucault, M. (1984) 'Nietzsche, Genealogy, History' in P. Rabinow (ed.), *The Foucault Reader*, London: Penguin: 76–100.

—— (1995) *Archaeology of Knowledge*, London: Routledge.
Francis, B. (2008) 'Engendering Debate: How to formulate a political account of the divide between genetic bodies and discursive gender?' *Journal of Gender Studies*, 17(3): 211–23.
—— (2010a) 'Re/theorising Gender: Female masculinity and male femininity in the classroom?' *Gender and Education*, 22(5): 477–90.
—— (2010b) 'Girls' Achievement: Contesting the positioning of girls as the relational "achievers" to "boys' underachievement"' in C. Jackson, C. Paechter and E. Renold (eds), *Girls and Education 3–16: Continuing Concerns, New Agendas*, Maidenhead: Open University Press: 21–37.
Frankland, J. and Bloor, M. (1999) 'Some Issues Arising in the Systematic Analysis of Focus Group Materials' in R. Barbour and J. Kitzinger (eds), *Developing Focus Group Research: Politics, Theory and Practice*, London: Sage: 144–55.
Frosh, S., Phoenix, A. and Pattman, R. (2002) *Young Masculinities: Understanding Boys in Contemporary Society*, Basingstoke: Palgrave.
Gans, H. (1974) *Popular Culture and High Culture: An Analysis and Evaluation of Taste*, New York: Basic Books.
Gauntlett, D. (2000) *Web.Studies: Rewiring Media Studies for the Digital Age*, London: Arnold.
—— (2007) *Creative Explorations: New Approaches to Identities and Audiences*, London: Routledge.
—— (2008) *Media, Gender Identity*, London: Routledge.
Gilbert, R. and Gilbert, P. (1998) *Masculinity Goes to School*, London: Routledge.
Gill, R. (2007) *Gender and the Media*, Cambridge: Polity Press.
Gill, R. and Scharff, K. (2011) *New Femininities: Neoliberalism and Subjectivity*, New York: Palgrave Macmillan.
Ging, D. (2005) 'A "Manual on Masculinity"? The consumption and use of mediated images of masculinity among teenage boys in Ireland' *Irish Journal of Sociology*, 14(2): 29–52.
Goffman, E. (1971) *The Presentation of Self in Everyday Life*, London: Pelican.
Gramsci, A. (1979) *Selections from the Prison Notebooks*, London: Lawrence & Wishart.
Griffin, C. (1985) *Typical Girls? Young Women from School to the Job Market*, London: Routledge & Kegan Paul.
—— (1993) *Representations of Youth: The Study of Youth and Adolescence in Britain*, Cambridge: Polity Press.
Grossman, A.H. and D'Augelli, A.R. (2007) 'Transgender Youth and Life-Threatening Behaviors' *Suicide and Life-Threatening Behavior*, 37(5): 527–37.
Guendouzi, J. (2001) '"You'll Think We're Always Bitching": The functions of cooperativity and competition in women's gossip' *Discourse Studies*, 3(1): 29–51.
Hains, R. (2012) *Growing Up With Girl Power: Girlhood on Screen and in Everyday Life*, Bern: Peter Lang Publishing.

Bibliography

Halberstam, J.J. (1998) *Female Masculinity*, Durham: Duke University Press.

—— (2005) *In a Queer Time and Place: Transgender Bodies, Subcultural Lives*, New York: New York University Press.

Hall, S. (2000) 'Who Needs "Identity"?' in P. Du Gay, J. Evans and P. Redman (eds), *Identity: A Reader*, London: Sage: 15–30.

Harris, A. (2004a) *Future Girl: Young Women in the Twenty-First Century*, London: Routledge.

—— (2004b) *All About the Girl: Culture, Power and Identity*, New York: Routledge.

Haywood, C. and Mac an Ghaill, M. (2012) '"What's Next for Masculinity?" Reflexive directions for theory and research on masculinity and education' *Gender and Education*, 24(6): 577–92.

Hesmondhalgh, D. (2005) 'Subcultures, Scenes or Tribes? None of the above' *Journal of Youth Studies*, 8(1): 21–40.

Hey, V. (1997) *The Company She Keeps: An Ethnography of Girls' Friendship*, Buckingham: Open University Press.

—— (2002) '"Not as Nice as she was Supposed to be": Schoolgirls' friendships' in S. Taylor (ed.), *Ethnographic Research: A Reader*, London: Sage (pp. 67–90).

Holmes, S. (2005) '"Starring... Dyer?" Re-visiting star studies and contemporary celebrity culture' *Westminster Papers in Communication and Culture*, 2(2): 6–21.

—— (2017) '"My Anorexia Story": Girls constructing narratives of identity on YouTube' *Cultural Studies*, 31(1): 1–23.

Hopkins, P. (2010) *Young People, Place and Identity*, London: Routledge.

Horrocks, J., House, A. and Owens, D. (2002) *Attendances in the Accident and Emergency Department following Self-harm: A descriptive study*. University of Leeds, Academic Unit of Psychiatry and Behavioural Sciences. https://www.mentalhealth.org.uk/a-to-z/s/self-harm#sthash.E0De8HFp.dpuf (accessed 29 August 2017).

Huppatz, K. (2009) 'Reworking Bourdieu's "Capital": Feminine and female capitals in the field of paid caring work' *Sociology*, 43(1): 45–66.

Jackson, R. and Dangerfield, C. (2002) 'Defining Black Masculinity as Cultural Property: Toward an identity negotiation paradigm' in L. Salmovar and R. Porter (eds), *Intercultural Communication: A Reader*, Belmont: Wadsworth: 120–30.

Järviluoma, H., Moisala, P., and Vilkko, A. (2003) *Gender and Qualitative Methods*, London: Sage.

Jenkins, R. (2002) *Pierre Bourdieu*, Abingdon: Routledge.

Karvonen, S., Young, R., West, P. and Rahkonen, O. (2012) 'Value Orientations among Late Modern Youth – A cross-cultural study' *Journal of Youth Studies*, 15(1): 33–52.

Kehily, M.J. (2002) *Sexuality, Gender and Schooling: Shifting Agendas in Social Learning*, London: Routledge Falmer.

—— (2004) 'Gender and Sexuality: Continuity and change for girls in school' in A. Harris (ed.), *All About the Girl: Culture, Power and Identity*, New York: Routledge: 205–16.

Keller, J. (2016) *Girls' Feminist Blogging in a Postfeminist Age*, New York: Routledge.

Kessler, S. and McKenna, W. (1978) *Gender: An Ethnomethodological Approach*, New York: John Wiley & Sons.

Korobkova, K. (2014) 'Schooling the Directioners: Connected learning and identity-making in the One Direction fandom' *Connected Learning Working Papers*, Irvine: Digital Media and Learning Research Hub.

Kozinets, R. (2010) *Netnography: Doing Ethnographic Research Online*, London: Sage.

Kundu, A. (2011) 'Understanding the Humanities' in A. Kundu and P. Naya (eds), *The Humanities: Methodology and Perspectives*, New Delhi: Longman: 1–19.

Laberge, S. (1995) 'Towards an Integration of Gender into Bourdieu's Concept of Cultural Capital' *Sociology of Sport Journal*, 12(2): 132–46.

Leung, A. and Kier, C. (2010) 'Music Preferences and Young People's Attitudes towards Spending and Saving' *Journal of Youth Studies*, 13(6): 681–98.

Lusher, D. and Robins, G. (2009) 'Hegemonic and Other Masculinities in Local Social Contexts' *Men and Masculinities*, 11(4): 387–423.

Mac an Ghaill, M. (1994) *The Making of Men: Masculinities, Sexualities and Schooling*, Buckingham: Open University Press.

Marshall, C. (1997) *Policy Analysis: A Perspective from Primary and Secondary Schooling*, London: The Falmer Press.

McCormack, M. (2011) 'Hierarchy without Hegemony: Locating boys in an inclusive school setting' *Sociological Perspectives*, 54(1): 83–102.

—— (2012) *The Declining Significance of Homophobia: How Teenage Boys are Redefining Masculinity and Heterosexuality*, Oxford: Oxford University Press.

McGrath, S.A. and Chananie-Hill, R.A. (2009) '"Big Freaky-Looking Women": Normalizing gender transgression through bodybuilding' *Sociology of Sport Journal*, 26(2): 235–54.

McGuffey, C.S. and Rich, B.L. (1999) 'Playing in the Gender Transgression Zone: Race, class, and hegemonic masculinity in middle childhood' *Gender and Society*, 13(5): 608–27.

McNay, L. (1999) 'Gender, Habitus and the Field: Pierre Bourdieu and the limits of reflexivity' *Theory, Culture & Society*, 16(1): 95–117.

McRobbie, A. (1991) *Feminism and Youth Culture: From "Jackie" to "Just Seventeen"*, Basingstoke: Macmillan Education.

—— (1994) *Postmodernism and Popular Culture*, London: Routledge.

—— (2009) *The Aftermath of Feminism: Gender, Culture and Social Change*, London: Sage.

Bibliography

Mendick, H., Allen, K., Harvey, L. and Ahmed, A. (2018) *Celebrity, Aspiration and Contemporary Youth*, London: Bloomsbury.

Messner, M. (1992) *Power at Play: Sports and the Problem of Masculinity*, Boston: Beacon Press.

Miles, S., Cliff, D. and Burr, V. (1998) '"Fitting In and Sticking Out": Consumption, consumer meanings and the construction of young people's identities' *Journal of Youth Studies*, 1(1): 81–96.

Modleski, T. (1984) *Loving with a Vengeance: Mass-Produced Fantasies for Women*, London: Methuen.

Moi, T. (1991) 'Appropriating Bourdieu: Feminist theory and Pierre Bourdieu's sociology of culture' *New Literary History*, 22(4): 1017–49.

Mori, M. (1970) 'The Uncanny Valley' *Energy*, 7(4): 33–5.

Myers, G. and Macnaghten, P. (1999) 'Can Focus Groups be Analysed as Talk?" in R. Barbour and J. Kitzinger (eds), *Developing Focus Group Research: Politics, Theory and Practice*, London: Sage (pp. 171–85).

Nayak, A. and Kehily, M.J. (1996) 'Playing it Straight: Masculinities, homophobias and schooling' *Journal of Gender Studies*, 5(2): 211–30.

—— (2006) 'Gender Undone: Subversion, regulation and embodiment in the work of Judith Butler' *British Journal of Sociology of Education*, 27(4): 459–72.

—— (2008) *Gender, Youth and Culture: Young Masculinities and Femininities*, Basingstoke: Palgrave Macmillan.

Oakley, A. (1972) *Sex, Gender and Society*, London: Maurice Temple Smith.

Ofsted (2012) *The Pupil Premium*, Manchester: Ofsted.

Orenstein, P. (2012) *Cinderella Ate My Daughter: Dispatches from the Front Lines of the New Girlie-girl Culture*, New York: HarperCollins.

Paechter, C. (2006) 'Masculine Femininities/Feminine Masculinities: Power, identities and gender' *Gender and Education*, 18(3): 253–63.

—— (2007) *Being Boys, Being Girls: Learning Masculinities and Femininities*, Maidenhead: Open University Press.

—— (2012) 'Bodies, Identities and Performances: Reconfiguring the language of gender and schooling' *Gender and Education* 24(2): 229–41.

Pedrozo, S. (2011) 'To be "cool" or not to be "cool": Young people's insights on consumption and social issues in Rio de Janeiro' *Journal of Youth Studies*, 14(1): 109–23.

Pomerantz, S. (2009) 'Between a Rock and a Hard Place: Un/defining the "girl"' *Jeunesse: Young People, Texts, Cultures*, 1(2): 147–58.

Prieur, A. and Savage, M. (2011) 'Updating Cultural Capital Theory: A discussion based on studies based in Denmark and Britain' *Poetics*, 39: 566–80.

Pringle, R. (2005) 'Masculinities, Sport, and Power: A critical comparison of Gramscian and Foucauldian inspired theoretical tools' *Journal of Sport & Social Issues*, 29(3): 256–78.

Radway, J. (1987) *Reading the Romance: Women, Patriarchy, and Popular Literature*, Chapel Hill: University of North Carolina Press.

Railton, D. (2001) 'The Gendered Carnival of Pop' *Popular Music*, 20(3): 321–31.

Rasmussen, M. (2004) '"That's So Gay!" A study of the deployment of signifiers of sexual and gender identity in secondary school settings in Australia and the United States' *Social Semiotics*, 14(3): 289–308.

Reay, D. (2001) '"Spice Girls", "Nice Girls", "Girlies", and "Tomboys": Gender discourses, girls' cultures and femininities in the primary classroom' *Gender and Education*, 13(2): 153–66.

Redman, P. (2000) 'The Subject of Language, Ideology and Discourse: Introduction' in P. Du Gay, J. Evans and P. Redman (eds), *Identity: A Reader*, London: Sage (pp. 9–14).

Renold, E. (1997) '"All They've Got on Their Brains is Football": Sport, masculinity and the gendered practices of playground relations' *Sport, Education and Society*, 2(1): 5–23.

—— (2005) *Girls, Boys and Junior Sexualities*, London: Routledge Falmer.

—— (2007) 'Tomboys and "female masculinity": (Dis)embodying hegemonic masculinity, queering gender identities and relations' in W. Martino, M. Kehler and M. Weaver-Hightower (eds), *The Problem With Boys: Beyond Recuperative Masculinity Politics*, New York: Sage (pp. 224–41).

Ringrose, J. (2011) 'Are You Sexy, Flirty or a Slut? Exploring "sexualization" and how teen girls perform/negotiate digital sexual identity on social networking sites' in R. Gill and C. Scharff (eds), *New Femininities: Postfeminism, Neoliberalism and Subjectivity*, New York: Palgrave Macmillan (pp. 99–116).

—— (2013) *Postfeminist Education? Girls and the Sexual Politics of Schooling*, London: Routledge.

Robb, M. (2007) 'Gender' in M.J. Kehily (ed.), *Understanding Youth: Perspectives, Identities and Practices*, London: Sage (pp. 107–46).

Roberts, S. (2012) '"I just got on with it": The educational experiences of ordinary, yet overlooked, boys' *British Journal of Sociology of Education*, 33(2): 203–21.

—— (2014) *Debating Modern Masculinities: Change, Continuity, Crisis?* Basingstoke: Palgrave Pivot.

Schilt, K. and Westbrook, L. (2009) 'Doing Gender, Doing Heteronormativity: "Gender normals", transgender people and the social maintenance of heterosexuality' *Gender & Society*, 23(4): 440–64.

Sichtermann, B. (1983) *Femininity: The Politics of the Personal*, Cambridge: Polity Press.

Scott, K. (2003) '"In Girls, Out Girls and Always Black: African-American girls' friendships' *Sociological Studies of Children and Youth*, 9: 179–207.

Serano, J. (2007) *Whipping Girl: A Transsexual Woman on Sexism and the Scapegoating of Femininity*, Emeryville: Seal Press.

Shary, T. (2002) *Generation Multiplex: The Image of Youth in Contemporary American Cinema*, Austin: University of Texas Press.

Bibliography

Silva, E. and Wright, D. (2005) 'The Judgement of Taste and Social Position in Focus Group Research' *Sociologia e ricerca sociale*, 76–7: 241–55.

—— (2008) 'Researching Cultural Capital: Complexities in mixing methods' *Methodological Innovations Online*, 2(3): 50–62.

Skeggs, B. (1997) *Formations of Class and Gender: Becoming Respectable*, London: Sage.

—— (2004a) 'Context and Background: Pierre Bourdieu's analysis of class, gender and sexuality' *The Sociological Review*, 52(2): 19–33.

—— (2004b) *Class, Self, Culture*, London: Routledge.

Skeggs, B. and Wood, H. (2008) 'The Labour of Transformation and Circuits of Value "around" Reality Television' *Continuum: Journal of Media and Cultural Studies*, 22(4): 559–72.

Slack, R. (1998) 'On the Potentialities and Problems of a WWW Based Naturalistic Sociology' *Sociological Research Online*, 3(2): n.p.

Smith, P.K., Madsen, K.C. and Moody, J.C. (1999) 'What Causes the Age Decline in Reports of being Bullied at School? Towards a developmental analysis of risks of being bullied' *Educational Research*, 41(3): 267–85.

Stewart, D., Shamdasani, P. and Rook, D. (2007) *Focus Groups: Theory and Practice*, London: Sage.

Stockton, K. (2009) *The Queer Child: Or Growing Sideways in the Twentieth Century*, Durham: Duke University Press.

Swain, J. (2000) '"The Money's Good, the Fame's Good, the Girls Are Good": The role of playground football in the construction of young boys' masculinity in a junior school' *British Journal of Sociology of Education*, 21(1): 95–109.

Thomas, A. (2004) 'Digital Literacies of the Cybergirl' *E-Learning*, 1(3): 358–82.

Thomas, M. (2008) 'Resisting Mothers, Making Gender: Teenage girls in the United States and the articulation of femininity' *Gender, Place & Culture*, 15(1): 61–74.

Thomson, R. and Holland, J. (2003) 'Hindsight, Foresight and Insight: The challenges of longitudinal qualitative research' *Social Research Methodology*, 6(3): 233–44.

Thorne, B. (1993) *Gender Play: Girls and Boys in School*, Buckingham, Open University Press.

Thornton, S. (1995) *Club Cultures: Music, Media and Subcultural Capital*, Cambridge: Polity Press.

Tolman, D. (2009) *Dilemmas of Desire: Teenage Girls Talk about Sexuality*, Cambridge: Harvard University Press.

Tyler, I. and Bennett, B. (2010) '"Celebrity Chav": Fame, femininity and social class' *European Journal of Cultural Studies*, 13(3): 375–93.

Vanderbeck, R., and Dunkley, C. (2003) 'Young People's Narratives of Rural–Urban Difference' *Children's Geographies*, 1(2): 241–59.

Veblen, T. (2007 [1899]) *The Theory of the Leisure Class*, Oxford: Oxford University Press.

Wald, G. (2002) '"I Want it that Way": Teenybopper music and the girling of boy bands' *Genders*, 35: np.
Walkerdine, V. (1997) *Daddy's Girl: Young Girls and Popular Culture*, Basingstoke: Palgrave Macmillan.
West, C. and Zimmerman, D. (1987) 'Doing Gender' *Gender & Society*, 1(2): 125–51.
Wetherell, M. and Edley, N. (1999) 'Negotiating Hegemonic Masculinity: Imaginary positions and psycho-discursive practices' *Feminism & Psychology*, 9(3): 335–56.
White, R. and Wyn, J. (2004) *Youth and Society: Exploring the Social Dynamics of Youth Experience*, Oxford: Oxford University Press.
Willett, R. (2011) 'An Ethnographic Study of Preteen Girls' Play with Popular Music on a School Playground in the UK' *Journal of Children and Media*, 5(4): 341–57.
Willis, P. (1978) *Learning to Labour: How Working Class Kids Get Working Class Jobs*, Aldershot: Ashgate.
Wilska, T.A. (2003) 'Mobile Phone Use as Part of Young People's Consumption Styles' *Journal of Consumer Policy*, 26(4): 441–63.
Wood, H. (2009) *Talking with Television: Women, Talk Shows and Modern Self-reflexivity*, Urbana: University of Illinois Press.

Index

10 Things I Hate About You, 35
50 Shades of Grey, 118
90210, 107, 118

Aapola, S., 101
Abbott, Diane, 2, 94
Alien vs. Predator, 109, 133
Anastasia, 26, 132
Anderson, Eric, 6, 74, 86, 123, 130, 147
Andersson, F., 79
Andre, Peter, 124, 125
Ang, I., 104, 105
Ashley, M., 80
Atencio, M., 131

Backstreet Boys, 112
Barker, G., 2, 79
Barry, P., 56
Bates, L., 2
Baumgardner, J., 101
Beatles, The, 90, 111, 112
Bennett, A., 142
Bennett, B., 116
Bennett, T., 5–6, 18, 22–3, 36, 81
Bieber, Justin, 90, 111, 114, 115, 121
Big Brother, 66, 118
Biklen, S.K., 13
Blackman, S., 17
Bloor, M., 24

Boberg, M., 21
'bonfire of the quangos', 153
Bourdieu, Pierre, 5, 6, 18, 22, 36, 45, 128, 142, 149
Breaking Bad, 83
Britain's Got Talent, 81
Brown, L.M., 122
Bryson, Bethany, 6, 7, 38, 143
Bulman, R.C., 36
Burr, 41
Butler, Judith, 36, 39, 55–7

Cann, V., 53, 112, 129
capital,
  cultural, 5–6
  economic, 5
  social, 5
Carrie, 35
Carter, C., 153
Chananie-Hill, R.A., 136
Cheng, C., 76, 83
cis, 57 *see also* cisgender
cisgender, 57
class, 5, 25, 45, 80, 100, 137–8, 142, 149, 158
Cliff, D., 41
Clueless, 35
Currie, D., 101
Connell, R., 74, 75, 80, 83, 105, 127, 145, 146
Connell, R.W., 59, 89
Coy, M., 117

Dangerfield, C., 128
Dare-Edwards, H.L., 112
D'Augelli, A.R., 2
David, M., 152
Day of the Girl, Norwich, 98
de Beauviour, S., 141
Dead Poets Society, 35
Delusions of Gender, 57
Disney, 26, 85, 132
Distinction, 142 *see also* Bourdieu
Doctor Who, 81, 84
Driscoll, C., 36, 101
Driver, Susan, 61, 120
Dunbar Jr, C., 12

Easy A, 35
Edley, N., 76
Ehrenreich, B., 112
Epstein, D., 7, 79, 120, 121
ethnography, 12, 13, 16–18
Euro 2012, 133
Evans, Abi, 19
Evans, Bethan, 59

Facebook, 1–2, 19
Faludi, S., 98
fangirling, 112, 133, 137–8, 147, 151
Fast Times at Ridgemont High, 35
feminine, femininity, 57, 100–5, 147, 148, 151
  hegemonic femininity, 100
  value, 104–6
feminism, 16, 73–4, 79, 97, 101, 102, 104, 105, 150–1, 158
  postfeminism, 98–9, 102, 117
Ferguson, A., 11
Fielding, N., 16
Fine, Cordelia, 57
fluidity, 55–6, 60, 62, 63, 71–2, 108, 119–20, 130, 145, 146, 150
  see also queer
football, 86, 132, 133, 134
Foucault, Michel, 55
Fox, Megan, 91, 93, 94, 115

Francis, Becky, 120, 145, 148, 150
Frankland, J., 24
Friends, 81
friendship(s), 47–9, 98, 129, 137
Frosh, S., 7, 43, 79, 91, 94, 131

Gans, R., 5
Game of Thrones, 83
Garner, M., 117
Gauntlett, D., 19, 23, 101
gender, 46, 48, 55, 63
  binary, binaries, 1, 3, 23, 55, 57–9, 61–2, 68–9, 82, 119–21, 139, 141, 150–1
  experience, 17
  Gendered Intelligence, 152
  neutral, 1
  performance, 59
  reproduction, 36–8
geographies, 2, 7, 13, 14, 15–16, 25, 62, 98, 131
Get Over It, 35
Gevinson, Tavi, 97
Ghost World, 35
Gilbert, P., 86, 94
Gilbert, R., 86, 94
Gill, Ros, 98, 99, 102, 104, 150
Ging, Debbie, 17, 79–80, 83
Glee, 65, 66, 72, 131
Goffman, Erving, 50, 59, 60, 125
Gonick, M., 101
Gramsci, A., 75, 100
Griffin, Christine, 12, 56, 101
Grossman, A.H., 2
Guendouzi, J., 43, 113

Hains, R., 2, 101
Halberstam, Jack J., 55, 118, 136, 148
Hall, Stewart, 56
Harris, A., 98, 99, 100, 101, 148
Haywood, C., 146
Heathers, 35
Hesmondhalgh, D., 4, 7, 71, 141
Hey, V., 17, 48, 101, 113

Index

Horrocks, J., 2
Holland, J., 25
Holmes, 116
Holt, Grant, 81
homohysteria, 77, 147
homophobia, 77–80, 118, 122, 126, 131, 143, 153
homosexualization, 79, 81
Hoolahan, Wes, 81
Hopkins, P., 16
Hot Fuzz, 133
House, A., 2
Hughes, John, 35
humour, 91, 93, 122, 128, 129, 130–1, 136
Hunger Games, The, 25
Huppatz, K., 6
hyper-regulation, 8, 9, 36, 38, 39–41, 44, 53, 60, 61, 68, 69, 72, 82, 89, 91, 94, 119, 120, 122, 126, 139, 141, 142–4, 146, 150, 151, 154, 156

identity, 55–9
Ingram, 74
Instagram, 2
International Day of the Girl Child, 98

Jackson, R., 128
Jackson, Simeon, 81
Järviluoma, H., 4, 12
Jenkins, R., 5
Johnson, R., 7, 79, 120, 121
Jonas Brothers, the, 90, 111
Jordan *see* Price, Katie

Kardashians *see Keeping up with the Kardashians*
Karvonen, S., 7
Keeping up with the Kardashians, 1
Kehily, Mary-Jane, 4, 7, 17, 56, 63, 68, 69, 71, 79, 94, 102, 113, 117
Keller, Jessalynn, 97, 99, 100, 101
Kelly, D., 101
Kessler, S., 121

Kidulthood, 81
Kier, C., 37
Korobkova, K., 112
Kozinets, R., 19
Kundu, A., 3

Lady Gaga, 55
Learning to Labour, 17
Lego, 1, 2
Leung, A., 37
LGB Youth, 70–1, 79, 93, 126, 136, 143, 146
Linkin Park, 90
Loose Women, 133
Lorenzo, Jorge, 1

Mac an Ghaill, M., 93, 121, 146
Macnaghten, P., 24
Madsen, K.C., 42
Marshall, C., 152
Martin, Ricky, 1
Martin, Russell, 81
masculinity, 57, 74–6, 80, 81, 95,
  hegemony, hegemonic masculinity, 74–6, 122, 126, 131, 138–9, 145–6
  hypermasculinity, 122, 126–9
  inclusive masculinities, 6, 74, 76–8, 79, 81, 123, 130, 146
  value of masculinity, 82
Mask You Live In, The, 73
Match of the Day, 81, 121
McCormack, M., 6, 7, 82, 105, 123, 130, 131
McGrath, S.A., 136
McGuffey, C.S., 121, 136
McKenna, W., 121
McRobbie, A., 4, 7, 11, 98, 99, 101
Mean Girls, 35
Messerschmidt, 89
Messi, Lionel, 81
Messner, M., 86
Miles, S., 41
Misfits, 110

171

Modleski, T., 104, 105
Moi, T., 38
Moisala, P., 4, 12
Monáe, Janelle, 55
Moody, J.C., 42
Morris-Roberts, 48
Mudhoney, 18, 38
Myers, G., 24

Napoleon Dynamite, 26
Nayak, Anoop, 4, 7, 56, 63, 65, 68, 69, 71, 79, 94, 102
Naylor, Joe, 19
neoliberal context, 73, 98
Newsom, Jennifer S., 73
Norris, Chuck, 83, 108

Oakley, Anne, 57
Ollila, E., 21
One Direction, 51, 90, 91, 111, 112, 114, 118, 121, 133, 138
Orange is the New Black, 55
Orenstein, P., 2, 101
Owens D., 2

Paechter, Carrie, 80, 100, 105, 118, 122, 136, 145, 148, 151
Paltrow, Gwyneth, 64
patriarchy, 6, 55, 57, 60, 69–71, 76, 99, 101–2, 105, 112, 118, 129, 136–8, 141
Parker, L., 12
Pattman, R., 7, 43, 79, 91, 94, 131
Phoenix, A., 7, 43, 79, 91, 94, 131
Piippo, P., 21
Policy Recommendations, 151–3
Pomerantz, S., 100, 101
Pretty Woman, 143
Price, Katie, 91, 92, 93, 94, 115, 116
Prieur, A., 5
Pringle, R., 77

queer, 62, 71, 72, 77, 108, 120, 121, 139, 150

Queer Theory, 8, 11, 57–60, 71, 137, 150
Queer Youth Cultures, 120 *see also* Driver, Susan

race, 1, 12, 14–15, 25, 73, 79, 80, 100, 131, 143, 149, 152, 155, 158
Radway, J., 81, 104, 105
Railton, D., 111
Rasmussen, M., 79
Reay, Diane, 132
Redtube, 133
Renold, E., 86, 113, 121, 148
resistance, 79, 129–31, 137–8
Rich, B.L., 121, 136
Richards, A., 101
Ringrose, J., 97–8, 101, 113, 116, 117, 121, 152
Ringwald, Molly, 35
Ritchie, Lionel, 130
Roberts, Steve, 2, 73, 80, 120, 146
Rodriguez, D., 12
Rook, D., 24
Rossi, Valentino, 1
Rushmore, 35

Savage, M., 5
Scharff, K., 99, 102, 104
Scott, K., 48
Second Sex, The, 141 *see also* de Beauvoir, S.
sex, 63
sexuality, 69
Shary, T., 36
Showunmi, V., 152
Sichterman, B., 115
Silva, E., 18, 19, 23–4
Skeggs, Beverley, 5, 6, 45, 116, 138, 142, 149
Slipknot, 18, 38
Smith, P.K., 42
Snapchat, 2
Snow Patrol, 90
'So This is Me', 21

Index

Spice Girls, 97
Steiner, L., 153
stereotyping, 3
Stewart, D., 24
Stockton, K., 11
Superbad, 35
Surman, Andrew, 81
Swain, J., 86

taste, 1, 38–9
  culture, 6–8, 17–18, 26, 40, 53, 92, 103, 112, 142
  and identity (re)production, 4–5, 9, 28, 36–8, 42–4, 46–51, 56, 61, 69, 74, 80, 87, 99, 102, 106, 111, 113–17, 120, 121–2, 138–9, 143, 144–8
  theory, 5–6, 19, 45, 142, 149
teachers, 13, 19, 152
Thomas, A., 22
Thomas, M., 100, 148
Thomson, R., 25
Thorne, B., 13, 42, 100
Thornton, S., 40, 45
Tierney, Marc, 81
Titanic, 85, 110
Tolman, D., 117
TransAmerica, 55
Turner, Frank, 90
Twilight, 42, 83, 118

Twitter, 114
Tyler, I., 116

Vampire Diaries, The, 124
Veblen, T., 5
Vilkko, A., 4, 12

Wald, G., 112
Walkerdine, V., 101
Walking Dead, The, 83, 84, 133
Waller, 74
West, C., 59
Wetherell M., 76
What's On TV, 29
Whitbread, Zak, 81
White, R., 7
Williams, Robin, 73–4
Willette, R., 111, 131
Willis, Paul, 16
Wilska, T.A., 37
Wood, Helen, 33, 56, 116
Wright, D., 18, 19, 24
Wright, J., 131
Wyn, J., 7

Youth Theory, 4, 7, 11, 12–13, 16–17, 94, 120
Yousafzai, Malala, 97

Zimmerman, D., 59, 60